First Edition 1996

© Bill Merrington 1996

Advantage,
The Town House,
46 Radford Road,
Leamington Spa,
Warwickshire
CV311LZ
Telephone: **01926 451521**

ISBN 0 9524809 5 6

Cover & Book Design by:
Mike Hughes,
Redhouse Studios,
3 Wavell Drive,
Rosehill, Carlisle,
Cumbria CA1 2ST
Telephone: 01228 43663

Printed & Bound in Great Britain by:
Howe of Brampton Limited,
Townfoot Industrial Estate,
Brampton,
Cumbria CA8 1SW
Telephone: 016977 2447

To my precious children

Katy, Peter and Toby

Suffering Love:
Coping with the death of a child

Bill Merrington

Acknowledgements

Over the past few years, I have had the opportunity of sharing with parents who suffer in love at the loss of their precious children. Many have allowed me to question them and enquire at some depth of their pain and grief. Others have allowed me the greatest privilege of all; to be alongside them at the point of their child's death. Such experiences leave one feeling extremely close to such parents in terms of emotion and respect.

I would like to thank all the parents who have enriched my own life, especially by enhancing my appreciation of my own children and educating me about the true meaning of bereavement.

I am grateful to my secretary, Ellen Griffin, who assisted with typing, and my parish, St. Paul's Church, Leamington Spa, who kindly have allowed me to neglect them for the sake of others.

Finally, I wish to thank my family, my wife Jane and my three children – Katy, Peter, and Toby – who have given me space and love to complete this work. I have often wondered, in the process of writing this book, of what it would be like for Jane and me to join the growing number of bereaved parents. At times I have felt the tears welling up in my eyes, yet I have always been able to draw back from the imagination and re-engage reality. I thank God for my family and pray I will enjoy them right into my old age.

Bill Merrington
Leamington Spa
October 1995

Contents

Foreword

For any parent the death of their child, or children, is an event riven with personal tragedy, pain and anguish. It is an experience which will leave its mark on those parents for the rest of their lives, as they face a future where so many of their dreams and aspirations will remain unfulfilled.

As a support organisation of bereaved parents, for bereaved parents, The Compassionate Friends is painfully aware that the path of parental grief is a long and difficult one, and recovery will, in all probability, take far longer than society expects, understands, or is willing to cope with. As time goes by the support systems of relatives, friends and those in the caring professions, so immediate and necessary after the death, begin for a variety of reasons to be around less often. This can leave bereaved parents feeling abandoned and isolated at the very time when they most need comfort, support and understanding. For those who have not experienced such a loss it is difficult to realise just how long it takes to grieve, and to adjust to the enormity of what has happened. Each individual's grief is unique, coming in waves and progressing erratically. There is no time limit to grief and in the early stages recovery seems to be impossible. Acceptance and eventual healing are not achieved in a matter of weeks, months or even years. What bereaved parents most need is an acknowledgement and an assurance that their reactions, feelings, fears and emotions are 'normal' given the tragic circumstances. To provide a 'cure' is an impossibility but with support and encouragement it is possible to come to the realisation that life, although it will never be the same again, can once more have meaning and hope.

The Reverend Bill Merrington demonstrates a deep and thoughtful understanding of the plight of bereaved parents. His personal experience as a maternity hospital chaplain and his more recent researches with bereaved parents themselves have combined to make the following chapters a realistic assessment of how bereaved parents think, feel and cope with their grief. For professional caregivers this is a practical and positive guide to the grief process experienced by bereaved parents, which will enable them to have a greater understanding and appreciation of the complexities surrounding the death of a child. The positive message throughout the book is that with love, care and support bereaved parents can learn to live with the pain of their loss. It will never go away but it is still possible to go forward to a new and meaningful life – there is a 'Way Ahead'.

Jenny Whitaker
Chairman
The Compassionate Friends

Introduction

The Reality of Childhood Death

She was like a china doll,

small and fragile. She was like

a kitten, mischievous and unpredictable.

She was like a forever-burning

candle bringing warmth and happiness

to whoever saw her.

Her skin was like silk and

she had a smile that made

everything seem better than it was. She was my daughter

and she will always be with me.

A young father after the death of his baby

Every day in our newspapers and on TV news we learn that someone somewhere has died. Whether it is war in Rwanda, Bosnia or the Middle East, (until recently) a bomb in Northern Ireland, or through accident, illness or old age, it seems part and parcel of life. However, the sudden death of a child makes society pause in shock. We reacted with horror at the murder of Jamie Bulger, and suffered with the parents of the children who died in the M40 mini-bus accident. We followed every moment of the search for three-year-old Rosie Palmer, who disappeared when she when to buy an ice-cream. We watched the hunt for the murderers of seven-year-old Sophia Hook, who was kidnapped from a tent in her Uncle's back garden, and fifteen-year-old Naomi Smith who was murdered in a playground as she went to post a letter. When Leah Betts collapsed after taking an ecstasy tablet, we shared her parents' agony. These deaths make the news. The impact is felt through the whole nation.

Somehow, it makes us all reflect on the fragility of life. The high profile the media give to violent deaths may seduce us into thinking that childhood deaths are rare. Sadly, that is far from the truth. Whether it is the loss of a baby through miscarriage or cot death, a child dying from leukaemia, or a teenager killed in a motor bike accident, the fact is that thousands of young people die each year.

How are we to cope with such losses? Parents don't know what to do; friends feel awkward and neighbours often want nothing to do with the situation. On top of this, the caring professionals – doctors, nurses or clergy – can feel they are failures as they are unable to prevent such premature deaths. There are hundreds, even thousands, of stories where families experience perhaps the most traumatic loss anyone can ever face, each family having to answer a range of questions unique to them. There are no easy answers for parents in such a position. They can only learn to live with their memories and push on into the unknown.

John and Sue

It was approaching Christmas and life was hectic in the Smith family. John and Sue's marriage was not the happiest at the time. John was at work till late while Sue, after a busy day herself at work, was coping with her son and daughter. Ann, who was seven, said she had a headache. She never really seemed to have been poorly, unlike her brother, so mum simply gave her a junior aspirin.[1] Over the next few hours Ann's pain became worse, with a rash and blistering in her mouth. By the next morning, Ann's skin was beginning to peel away from her body. She had developed a rare toxic skin disease. The first week was critical, but Ann seemed to be holding her own. However, her parents had been told to expect the worst. After ten days, Ann seemed to be recovering when she had a fit and died suddenly from a heart attack. She had been released from her agony, but the family pain was only just beginning.

How can a family cope with such a loss? Whatever problems families have before a child dies, it is clear that they will carry such difficulties with them into the future. How do parents relate to each other when they seem to grieve in different ways? Is it possible to prevent the guilt and worry from affecting the other children in the family?

Fred and Alice

It was the first time Fred and Alice had left their son alone in the house for a weekend – the first real break for the parents in nineteen years. Fred and Alice were glad to get away from the constant family squabbles. Their eldest son, Ian, was busy working and wouldn't be at home much that weekend anyway. The younger son was going to stay with friends. Ian had a motor bike which was the real worry in the parents' lives. How many times had Ian heard them say, 'Be careful!' When Fred and Alice returned home from a magnificent weekend, they were relieved to see the motor bike safe in the garage. Seconds later, however, they discovered their son in the bathroom – dead from a drug overdose.

---

[1] Since this time, the dangers of giving aspirin to children under twelve have been well publicised, and all junior aspirin products withdrawn from the market.

When parents see all their hard work in parenting over many years disappear in seconds, can they ever recover? What do you do when you have a house full of belongings relating to your dead child? How do you react when you have relatives who cannot relate to your loss?

Alan and Martha

Alan and Martha were full of hope. Life had been tough, building up their own business. Despite the recession, they had survived, and now their son David, aged twenty-six, had finally decided to join the company. Even the shop-floor workers were pleased, for they hoped the son would secure the future of the business. David was married with a baby daughter. A keen cyclist, each day he would cycle to work, with Alan not far behind in his car. This day Alan had noticed an ambulance on the dual-carriageway but had thought nothing of it. By the time he had arrived at work, his son was dead. A car had ploughed straight into David's bike, killing him instantly. What would be the outcome for this family now? Would the business survive? How would David's wife cope with her life now, with a baby and parents-in-law destroyed by grief? How would the grandparents cope if their daughter-in-law remarried?

The Parent/Child Relationship

Parents who lose a child are in fact multiple victims.

> *We are victimised by the realistic loss of the child we love, we are victimised by the loss of the dreams and hopes we had invested in that child, and we are victimised by the loss of our own self-esteem. Not unlike the survivors of the concentration camps, we cannot comprehend why we did not die instead.[2]*

Much of parental identity centres around doing things for one's children, a basic function of the parent. Parents who have fulfilled the roles of provider, problem solver, protector and adviser, and who have been accustomed to being self-sufficient and in control, must now confront the interruption of these roles and the severing of the relationship with the child. The death of a child robs parents of their ability to carry out their functional roles, leaving them with an overwhelming sense of failure and attacking their sense of power and ability. Parents find themselves losing not only their child, but also their role in life, their future hopes and in some cases their loved ones around them.

Throughout the world today thousands of children are starving. Many young children have to work to support their families and provide food. However, in the modern Western world the status of children has been raised to a prominent position. At the beginning of the century it

---

[2] A S Kliman, quoted in Linzer, ed: *Understanding Bereavement and Grief.*, Yeshiva Press, New York, 1977.

was still common to have large families, on the premise that one or two children would die young from common diseases. In these large families, children were expected to be seen but not heard.

Today we have a very different situation. Children – of whatever age – are big business. A typical family is likely to consist of one to three children whose parents fully expect that their children will not only live to adulthood but will outlive them. On top of this, children play a far greater role in family life; they are definitely both seen and heard! There are so many activities available for children simply transporting them to events can be a time-consuming role for mums and dads. Children now mean big business in the world of clothing and toys and have therefore become targets for advertising on television and radio. All of this puts pressure on parents to get things right. We are now living in a more mobile society where families find themselves living miles away from other relatives. This creates the tendency to build one's life around the smaller family unit, putting greater emphasis on the parent-child bond. This is exacerbated when there is breakdown of relationships, creating one-parent families. Here the child can end up playing the role of friend and partner to the lonely parent. Thus, when tragedy does occur, resulting in the death of a child, the impact on the family is devastating and their structured lives crumble beneath them.

> *In a symbolic way, the death of a child represents the death of the self. Symbolically, a mother or father will die along with the child, only to survive in a damaged state with little or no desire to live today or plan for tomorrow.*[3]

Such deaths are seen as inappropriate, unnatural and unacceptable to parents. Families experience not only the loss of a loved one but also the loss of support. Society at large seems poorly equipped to support families in loss. Today, most deaths take place in hospital, which means there is no longer the neighbour at hand who has experience to share. Older relatives are often not near enough to be of help. There is also a tendency in our society to focus only on that which is successful and rewarding in life. Therefore it is not uncommon to find people distancing themselves from the bereaved almost as if death is contagious.

Displaying grief

Displaying emotion seems to be discouraged in the British culture, which limits bereaved parents' ability to express how they really feel. When they fail to return to what is called a 'normal life style,' many friends and neighbours lose interest in offering support. Although much has been written generally about the subject of bereavement, there is still the tendency for society to assume that bereaved parents should be back to normal, certainly one year after the death. However, we fail to see the turmoil and pain that is only just beginning to surface after one or two years of grief. Parents' feelings of grief tend to flow back and forth.

---

[3] R Knapp, *Beyond Endurance*, Schochen, New York, 1986.

It is rather like the tide coming in and out each day. Each time the tide comes up the beach you don't know what it will leave behind as it recedes. One day anger, another time depression, another outbursts of grief.[4]

Each individual will enter grief differently. There are many variables in a person's life which play a part in how they will grieve. Therefore, one must not stereotype people's reactions. It sometimes seems that counsellors and carers almost force a fake reaction from a bereaved person to fit in with their theory of what stage that person should have reached. The stages of the grieving process are not separate:

. . . they are invariably intertwined and overlap. Nor are they successive . . . or in any order. Shock customarily intones the grieving process, while establishment, if reached, means grief is over. The in-between stages vary in almost every conceivable way. Certain stages can be by-passed altogether, while others may last no longer than a few minutes. Highly charged feelings like anger are frequently more like flashes than emotional states, and softer emotions like sadness can remain as permanent features in the post-grief personality. . . . Only the practised eye can accurately discern the dominant themes at work and know readily the pressing needs of the griever.[5]

Many parents find they are still encountering grief symptoms years later. This is 'shadow grief' – remnants of powerful feelings.[6] Parents carry this weight within themselves for years, in some cases even for a lifetime.

The problems that parents encounter raise questions not only for themselves but for the whole community. How can we care for someone who has experienced something we are all terrified of encountering?

Moreover, how can we care for someone when we have no answers to give to their unending questions? Those who give glib answers quickly find the bereaved parents are sharp at identifying the shallowness of such answers. They are not interested in false or easy explanations. To say that the loss of a child at any age is 'not so bad' is an insult to the parent. A father who lost his twenty-five year-old son in a climbing accident said:

Death is awful, demonic. If you think your task as a comforter is to tell me that really, all things considered, it's not so bad, you don't sit with me in my grief but place yourself off in the distance away from me. Over there you are of no help. What I need to hear from you is that you recognise how painful it is. I need to hear from you that you are with me in my desperation.[7]

---

[4] I Ainsworth-Smith, *Letting Go*, SPCK, London, 1982.

[5] R Kavanaugh, *Facing Death*, Penguin Books, Baltimore, 1974.

[6] Knapp, *op. cit.*

[7] N Wolterstorff, *Lament for a Son*, Eerdmans, Grand Rapids, 1987.

When lightning strikes twice

'I was told not long after losing my daughter that my son had cancer. Lightning does strike twice.'

When we say, 'Lightning never strikes twice,' we try to convince ourselves that we should not have to experience tragedy more than once. Nevertheless, I have met several parents whose experience causes them to disagree!

Perhaps the most common experience of multiple tragedy is when mothers have a series of babies die after almost full-term pregnancies. One mother had lost two babies at birth only to lose the third child through an accident before she was two years old. The pain of such events is beyond words. Parents tell themselves that they could not possibly handle another loss, yet somehow they do, and many go on to have children who see them into old age. Such parents can appear to those around them to be foolish to put themselves through such worrying times. Yet what they need most is the encouragement of friends around them, supporting them whatever the outcome.

However, where a family has lost more than one grown-up child the effects are devastating. A permanent numbness seems to remain for these parents who feel they have lost all they endeavoured to achieve.

Tragedy can come in a variety of forms. It is common to find that the loss of a grandchild is just too much for an elderly grandparent. Grandparents seem to feel it is a great injustice when they – who have lived a long and full life and are ready for death – find their grandchild, 60 or 70 years younger than they are, robbed of life. Grandparents often wish they could take the place of their grandchild to ease not only their own pain but the pain of their children. Some seem unable to accept such a loss and give up the will to live.

'Months later, my father died, he seemed to just give up the fight. He felt it should have been him, not his granddaughter.' ·

The loss of other loved ones, even of those who are elderly and ready to die, simply adds salt to an open wound. Any death is a catastrophe: however, the grief caused by the death of a loved one can differ in degree, depending on the expectations of the relationship. When a parent who is in pain from the loss of a child also loses a parent, it somehow deepens both losses, making the survivor feel more alone and isolated.

Even though their questions are unanswerable, many bereaved parents embark on a search for the answers they seek. Some look for it in established religion, or in mediums who claim to deliver messages from the dead; others seek meaning by caring for others in loss and supporting charities. In the meantime, they live with the knowledge that their pain is deeply tied to their love. They have loved their child and still love, so the suffering of the loss continues.

Why should I write a book about something I myself have not experienced? Some parents may say I have no right. It is true that many parents find it helpful to write about their experience and I am sure such books are a source of support for others in loss. Although in a sense I am an outsider, I have found myself sitting alongside many parents in their sad loss. As a hospital chaplain at Birmingham Maternity Hospital I was on call to draw alongside the parents when a miscarriage or stillbirth had taken place, or in the neo-natal unit to support parents as the battle for life was acknowledged to be lost and the hi-tech breathing equipment was switched off. I must have sat in a small room with a mum, dad and their tiny baby scores and scores of times. To be in a privileged position of intimacy alongside the parents as we waited for death's arrival, was in one sense the hardest job in my life, yet at the same time the most rewarding.

Since then, as a parish priest, I have found myself meeting, often for the first time, parents who have only hours previously lost their child. Although all ministers encounter such pastoral situations, I have met more than most. I have also seen several friends and contemporaries endure the experience of losing a baby through cot death, when I had small children at home. It was because of this experience and the constant echo of parents saying that they felt people did not understand them that I decided to undertake research into parents' reactions in order to achieve a better understanding of how to care for them appropriately.

I want to convey a message in this book that bereaved parents will identify with and to point out the similarities in peoples' experiences. If parents I have listened to feel I have represented their views, I will have achieved my aim, along with opening all of our eyes to the pain some of our neighbours and friends still carry.

Section One

Parents' Experiences

Nothing seems so devastating as the death of a child. In a society where people are surviving into their 80s and 90s, we are developing a system of coping with their deaths. We see it as a release from the pain of old age; with thanksgiving we are able to let them pass from life into death. However, when a young child dies it seems to catch society unawares. When a mother has a miscarriage, few people may be aware of the situation. But when a baby or young child dies people react with great shock. Somehow there seems to be no justification for the loss of an innocent child.

During pregnancy, parents are naturally worried for the development of the child, especially if it's their first child. Even after giving birth, a mother is extremely vulnerable as she adjusts suddenly to having hands-on experience, not with any child but with her own precious baby. Immediately after giving birth she must learn how to breast feed, change a nappy, and cope with a baby crying – all of this often in an open ward among other mothers and experienced nurses. Once home alone it's all up to her – no one else is responsible. However vulnerable that may make parents feel, the newness soon wears off as they get into a busy routine with their child. Assumptions take place in the parents' minds. Before birth it is the expectation that all will be well and the child will look like them. Once the baby is born, parents naturally assume that he or she will be a permanent fixture in their lives.

As we journey through life with our children, our assumptions of what we expect from them begin to change. We expect to give babies lots of physical holding and cuddles. It is an opportunity to give totally to the child as we feed, clothe and protect it. We are a twenty-four hour influence in our babies' lives. Later we expect to provide education, enabling our children to develop their abilities and gifts. We now begin to expect hugs and kisses from them. As our children become teenagers and young adults our expectations are still prominent in the relationship. We now look for friendship, the recognition that our children like us. As we begin to shape their lives less, we also gradually assume they will be around to care for us. Indeed, our work and careers continue into our latter years, aiming to help our children later in life as they support us. All through our years with our children, the one abiding assumption is that they will be around us. The assumptions that we formulate, however sub-consciously, play a key role in how we cope with loss when the child dies.

1

Research into Parents' Experiences

We seem to give them back to you,

you who gave them to us.

Yet you did not lose them by giving them to us,

so we do not lose them by their return to you.

What you give us, you never really take away,

life is eternal and love is immortal.

And death is only an horizon,

and an horizon is nothing but the limit of our vision.

Anonymous

A carer wants to get as close as possible in his or her understanding of a situation, yet never wants to experience the actual pain itself. I have talked to many parents who have said they felt that the professional did not understand what they were going through. In one sense this is understandable, for with each death, the feeling of bereavement is unique to the individuals involved. However, we can learn from the similarities in people's experience. The danger is that we take a general opinion about bereavement and transfer it to the whole population. This creates anger in parents who feel that people around them have not listened to how they truly feel and therefore have failed to understand them.

I acknowledge from the outset that, both as an outsider to bereavement and as one who is looking for similarities in people's situations, I may well fall into my own trap. However, the more we can understand bereavement in various situations, the more widely the subject can be discussed, and hopefully the more sensitive we become to the individual's needs.

One area where research into bereavement has been overlooked is in families who have lost children:

- ❤ Do parents react differently according to the age of the child who died?

- ❤ Are the long-term effects of loss greater for those who have lost young children, compared to those who have lost teenagers or young adults?

- ❤ Can one say there is an age at which death causes less or more tragedy in a family?

Having come into contact with a range of parents in bereavement, I wanted to investigate whether there were any common factors in the bereavement process and to seek the most appropriate ways to care for people in grief. To obtain relevant data for this research, I interviewed around one hundred parents scattered throughout England. To identify participants I approached bereaved parents in my own parish and contacted the local co-ordinators of The Compassionate Friends. I asked if they would establish whether parents who had lost a baby, child, teenager or young adult were willing to participate in a study. I telephoned potential participants and outlined what I intended. This gave them an opportunity to think about my request before accepting or refusing. This was important, because all those who decided to assist found the process, although helpful, extremely upsetting too. The main reason for the parents' participation in a study which would be intensely painful at times was the desire to provide information that would be helpful to parents and their surviving children in similar situations in the future.

All interviews took place pivataely in the homes of the subjects so that they could feel relaxed, relate to the environment of their lost child, and allow me to enquire fully into the bereavement situation. To protect confidentiality, the incidents I have described and the quotations I have used are composites. The grief expressed, however, is real.

It is a privileged position to meet parents for the first time and hear over a period of two hours or more their own story of their child's death. Before each interview I asked parents to complete two questionnaires, the Grief Experience Inventory[8] and the Parental Inter-relationship Questionnaire. Since bereavement is multidimensional, it is not easy to assess its intensity in an individual. These two questionnaires provided information for a subjective analysis. A few parents felt unable to complete the questionnaires because they found them too impersonal. The interview followed a framework of structured questions covering how the family functioned before the child's death, at the point of death, and days, months, and years later. Participants were encouraged to discuss their own grief experience and events surrounding the death of their child. Most interviews were audio-taped but on a few occasions I took handwritten notes.

---

[8]C.M. Sanders, P.A. Mauger and P N Strong Jr, The Grief Experience Inventory, Consulting Psychologists Press, Palo Alto, 1985.

Major Findings

Analysis of the impact of loss in parents through the questionnaires and interviews showed that:

- The age of a child plays a key role in the rate of recovery of a parent.

- Parents share common experiences, and frequently suffer long lasting 'shadow grief'.

- The type of death affects parents, particularly where suicide takes place.

- The death of a child affects the whole family unit.

- The role of Christian churches was supportive at first, but rather weak at caring long term.

- Friends proved more supportive than relatives.

- Support groups, provided they did not become too claustrophobic, proved very beneficial.

The age of the child

Parents who lost younger children reacted less strongly than parents grieving for older teenagers and young adults. However, those losing children up to the age of two years felt isolated because they lost the social contact that mothers experience when they have young children. Whether at the playgroup, nursery or school, parents in the early days of parenthood spend a large portion of their time in situations with other parents. When a loss occurs, this regular meeting point is removed.

Since parents who lose 0 – 2-year-olds are generally younger than those who lose older children, a higher percentage are able to have another child. Over two-thirds of of parents bereaved of children under 10 years old said they later had another child, whereas for parents who had lost a child 18 years or over it was less than a quarter. Hence the impact of bereavement was differed for younger families.

Nearly ninety per cent of parents said they included the dead child when asked how many children they had in the family. Of those whose child had before the age of two years, 75% included that child during the first two years of loss. However, after two years the figure dropped to 26%. Older parents who were unable have more children were more likely to ruminate on the situation, and since an older child has played a larger part in the family life, he or she is more likely to be included in the family even though deceased.

There was a greater sense of hope in families who had lost younger children rather than teenagers, except where, for physical reasons, the younger families were unable to have more children.

With parents of older children there were hidden factors which seemed to prolong the grief process. Friction in the family unit seemed greater in older families, whose members were carrying a greater degree of guilt and anger. Often with older children, there have been times of disagreement or upset perhaps over a girlfriend or a job, or just the state of a bedroom. These points of friction stick in parents' minds and create in them long-lasting guilt.

'I feel guilty that all the worry I had over my teenage son has now gone.'

'There were so many problems unresolved.'

'I wish I'd not pushed him to get a job now.'

A father who lost a $15^1/2$ year-old daughter expressed his anger by saying, 'Anyone who has lived over $15^1/2$ years has had a life.' This father felt strongly that his daughter's life had never really started.

Parents share common grief experiences, which last longer than expected

All parents have a tendency to hold on to past events, to dream of their children, and to agonise about what to do with their possessions. Anger, guilt and even thoughts of suicide are common. The feeling of bereavement lasted longer than expected, particularly with teenage loss. Many parents are still experiencing 'shadow grief' as much as 20 years after their child's death. They describe this as a dull ache in the background of one's feelings that remains fairly constant and which, under certain occasions, comes bubbling to the surface, whether with tears or not, but accompanied by a feeling of sadness and a mild sense of anxiety. The term was created by L G Peppers and R Knapp[9] who found the lingering effects of grief to be quite prominent among mothers who suffered perinatal losses. In such cases, mothers never seemed completely able to shake off the vestiges of grief and remnants remained for years.

This does not mean that grief continues to dominate bereaved parents' existence as it once did, but rather that the experience of the child's death and many of the attendant feelings do remain, ever so subtly, and perhaps are never entirely forgotten or resolved. Of all of those interviewed, 61% of the parents said they had problems still to resolve, but with the loss of teenagers the figure was 82%. Of those interviewed who had been bereaved ten years or more, 60% felt they still had problems to resolve because of the death. When asked whether they had fear of further loss in their life, 40% of those bereaved over 10 years ago answered positively. It is important for parents to understand the concept of 'shadow grief' so that they can accept their behaviour as normal for bereaved families.

---

[9] R Knapp, *Beyond Endurance*, New York, Schochen, 1986

The type of death

In the analysis of parents, 60% were bereaved through illness, 33% through accidents and 5% through suicide. Families where the death was caused through accident displayed more anger than ones whose child died from illness. Blame for accidental death could usually be specifically directed. When death occurs suddenly, it leaves more repercussions for the parents. Death due to accidents, such as motor bike accidents, can leave the parents angry for the part the teenager played in the death. This is especially the case if death occurs because of misuse of drugs or a sexual experiment that goes wrong. Parents also have strong feelings of anger towards those who encouraged the child to venture down this path.

With illness it is harder for parents to focus their anger at a particular person. Where children have died in ways that might have been preventable, blame can be high on the agenda for one of the partners. This might arise, for example, if one partner had hereditary problems which were passed on to the child, thus contributing to its death.

Anger seems to surface more in the first year, especially in men. Guilt was dominant in parents whose child had committed suicide. All the parents who acknowledged they had experienced a nervous breakdown came from the group whose loss was sudden. This highlights the issue of anticipatory grief which can assist bereavement. When death is preceded by a prolonged illness, parents can exhibit a variety of reactions which echo bereavement symptoms. Where death had been sudden, parents felt they had been robbed, whereas parents who had nursed a child for weeks and months afterwards expressed great satisfaction and pleasure in caring for their child. It provided an opportunity, particularly for the mother, to become as intimate again with their loved child as they were at birth or in the child's early life.

When diagnosis is wrong or delayed and a mother is told to stop fussing only to discover later how serious the illness is, the result is understandable anger which lingers for years. One mother had been told by a health visitor and her GP to stop wasting their time with supposed minor baby problems; four months later the consultant who saw the baby immediately asked, 'Why haven't I seen you before?' and diagnosed a serious genetic disorder. The parents subsequently changed doctors but carried their anger with them.

Where the medical care has gone smoothly before the child's death, parents generally recall such times with positive thankfulness, but if there has been any miscommunication the events stick in the parents' minds. Having driven over 100 miles with their child for a diagnosis, one couple was told that their child had less than 12 months to live and left to drive back in shock without counselling. Obviously, when parents recall instances of unhappiness one must acknowledge that the hospital personnel may have a very different view of the story. However, it is the perception the parents are left that bereavement counsellors have to deal with.

When illness is prolonged, parents can adjust their reactions from disbelief to distancing themselves from the child. Reactions can be complex. Fathers appear able to remove themselves from the intensity of care. They often have to go out to work, leaving the twenty-four hour care to mum, whose role means she loses her job, her friends and eventually her child. Several fathers confessed to this distancing and now regret not being closer to their child. Mothers' reactions can also be mixed at such times. One mother of a baby with a rare genetic illness said:

> *'I never wanted to lose her, but equally I never wanted her like this. Some days I would be okay, but others I wanted to throw the baby in the bin.'*

Mothers can feel trapped either at home or in hospital with their child.

> *'I felt everyone knew it was a genetic problem so I was embarrassed. I felt trapped at home like a freak.'*

Many parents remember the day of diagnosis more clearly than the day of death.

> *'The day of diagnosis was the day grief and bereavement began.'*

Effect on the whole family unit

Whatever a couple's relationship is like before the loss of a child, afterwards it is likely to change. Parents may assume that since they have shared such a great tragedy together, helping each other to recover will draw them together. This does sometimes happen. With some parents there is no obvious change, but with others existing problems are made worse or new ones created. The analysis showed that marriages were generally weakened. Fewer than 7% of parents said that a partner helped to fill the gap left by the child. For those 6 – 10 years on since loss, half said their marriage had deteriorated. Thirty-seven per cent of parents said they now spend less time together, and almost half said their sex life had deteriorated.

Siblings, who often feel neglected, have long lasting problems. Overall, the loss of a brother or sister seems to have a major negative effect on peoples' lives. This is an area that needs further study. In general, siblings are hesitant about speaking of the deceased for months and in some cases years. However, most seem to recover the normality of their lives even if educational development is put back for a while. Some react more severely, either becoming extremely extrovert in character or withdrawing into themselves. A few seem to seek out partners with a resemblance to their dead brother or sister – a sense of finding a replacement, but often with negative results. Others move away from the family, perhaps to escape the claustrophobic atmosphere but this only serves to increase parental worries.

At work, parents' previous ambitions and motivation are sapped. When one married partner works, while the other remains at home, a sense of disharmony is often created. In the questionnaires, 16% said they were less motivated at work. However, 30% did not answer the question. In the interviews, over 50% mentioned difficulty at work. Only one man expressed a wish for success, and even here it was to provide for his other children's education, which had become important to him.

Role of Christian churches

The number of people who attended the funeral was the greatest comfort to parents, rather than the Christian message conveyed. When parents were asked what part of the funeral service was most comforting, 48% said the number of people present. But with the loss of an 11 – 18 year old, this figure increased to 71%.

All the parents interviewed, when asked whether the funeral helped them in any specific way, said some of the service was a blur. However, 58% of the parents said the funeral was a comfort. If the minister or funeral director made an error in the proceedings, then the parents would recall it, but if the ceremony went smoothly most of the kind words merged together, comforting and helping them to get through the ritual. Generally, parents held on to the concept of God and the after-life but modified their view of God's omnipotence.

Support from friends

Close-knit communities were better able to face the loss. Larger communities seem to uphold the conspiracy theory of ignoring the loss, once the funeral was over. Parents do not bounce back to be themselves after a few months. It is after the early months, when some get tired of caring, that a few close friends can provide the most support. To be willing to mention the unmentionable – the dead child's name – a year after its death is unusual, yet parents still want to talk about their child. Many people tend to think that it is better not to upset a parent by mentioning the child. However, the parents are already upset and becoming disturbed that there seems to be a conspiracy of silence around them. Although talking about the deceased may cause a few tears, these are tears parents are only too willing to shed. Of the parents interviewed, only 12% said they had ever avoided the opportunity to talk about their child or had generally avoided people, yet half felt that people had avoided them.

Benefits of support groups

Support groups proved to be very beneficial, provided they did not become too claustro-phobic. Parents were relieved to meet other people with similar experiences. The knowledge that others also encountered such depths of despair, along with real physical pain, yet survived, encouraged parents. In support groups, bereaved parents can meet others who have endured and survived and this gives them hope for themselves.

There are complex reasons why some parents join support groups while others stay away. Character and temperament have an influence. Individuals who attended generally felt supported and helped when their partners went with them. Where one partner refused to talk about the loss, the support group became the place for the other partner to share their feelings openly.

Some parents found it difficult to withdraw from the support group when they felt it had served its purpose. They had made friends and become carers, so felt it difficult to stop attending without feeling they were 'letting the side down'. However, those who attended felt that the positive benefits far outweighed the minor problems they encountered.

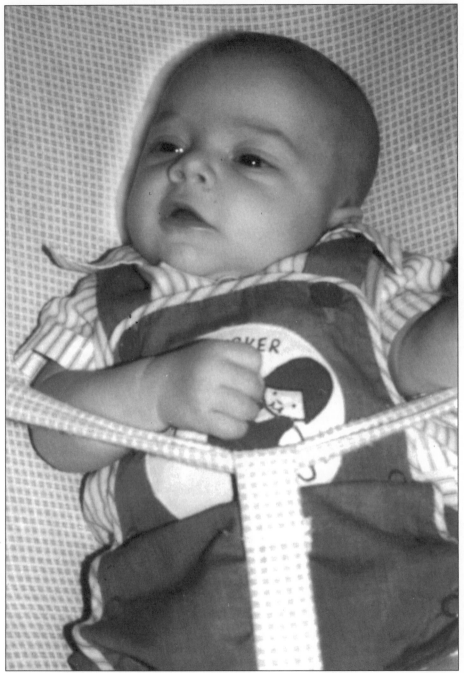

Simon at four months, a few weeks before his mother found him dead in his cot.

2

Miscarriage, Stillbirth, and Infant Death

We had our little baby girl.
We never brought you home.
We have no little hands to hold,
No pretty hair to comb.

Now our dreams are all we have
Of how you would have grown,
The places we'd have taken you,
The love we would have known.

If tears could turn to rain drops
And thoughts become a storm
There wouldn't have been a sunny day,
Since the day that you were born.

We love and miss you very much,
Is all we have to say.
You're in our thoughts,
You're in our hearts.

(A mother whose baby lived for thirty minutes — 1989)

Miscarriage

George and Rachel were looking forward to the birth of their second child. Rose was only three when her mum became pregnant again, but she picked up her parents' excitement. All went well for the first 18 weeks, until Rachel noticed that she could not feel any kicking in the womb. At first her GP felt there was nothing wrong and Rachel was making a fuss. Eventually however, the hospital gave Rachel another scan and very quickly she found herself having an emergency caesarean operation. By the time Rachel came round from the anaesthetic her baby had died. She was still in a daze when she was allowed to hold her baby girl. The hospital took photographs, but it was all too much for Rachel to take in. Over the next couple of days she felt safe in hospital, in a small room on her own. Unfortunately, one nurse came into the room and asked, 'Where's your baby?' Rachel just could not stop crying. The baby girl was buried in her grandfather's grave after a service in the hospital chapel. Only the immediate family were present. Those around Rachel tried to support her by saying what they thought was right.

> *'Someone said to me, 'Are you better now?' as if it was a cold. Another person said, 'At least you didn't get to know it.' I felt like hiding in the house. You have months of preparation for the birth and suddenly it was all gone. I'd just assumed that the doctor would be able to make the baby better.'*

Rachel lost a stone in weight over the first year and began to worry about losing Rose, who ended up having counselling two years later. However, George and Rachel did find that other people began to talk to them about their own experiences of losing babies.

Four years later the couple had another child, although the pregnancy was an extremely worrying time for both. Rachel joined a self-help group called Stillbirth and Neonatal Death Society (SANDS). There she was able to share experiences with other mums.

> *'I still think about her every day. She would have been at school by now. I try and imagine what she would be like. I guess I idolise her in a way.'*

A miscarriage or spontaneous abortion is the unintended ending of a pregnancy before the time the foetus could survive outside the mother. This usually occurs before the 20th to 22nd week of pregnancy. Although miscarriage is common, the grief associated with it is often misunderstood (as is the grief associated with abortion – whatever society's attitude towards this might be). Since the baby has not been seen or recognised by other relatives and friends, there is the assumption that the pain of loss is not great. How often mums are told, 'You've been spared from an imperfect baby, don't worry, you can always have another.' However, the baby can be perfect, and for the parents it is not another baby they want but this one!

We still hears stories about mothers not being allowed to see the dead baby. Such situations cause great problems and pain. The mother's mind is able to create grotesque pictures and this can induce fear in mothers who never see their child. They assume the baby's deformities were alarming but most mothers are well able to cope with seeing their own baby, however deformed. I met a mother who had been carrying twins, but one of the babies died several weeks early in the womb. After birth, there was little to see of the remains of the dead baby, but when the mother was finally allowed to see it she immediately sensed a likeness to her healthy child. We took photographs which she was pleased to keep. Parents need freedom to choose.

A common reaction to miscarriage is nagging fear and the continual question, 'How did this happen?' Since the baby was so much part of the mother's physical body, it is natural for her to blame herself. Was it a result of lack of sleep, smoking, drinking, sexual intercourse, curry, not stopping work early enough, her age? The list of possible factors a mother can contemplate is endless. She may also wonder whether the hospital made a mistake, and in some cases show anger towards the GP, who kept saying everything was okay, and towards the Health Visitor, who made her feel she was just a fussing pregnant lady.

For many, having a child is a sign of being a normal human being. Therefore, when it seems to go wrong, mothers can have strong negative feelings about themselves. They have no control over the loss, so they feel helpless. On top of this, they have been nurturing a source of expectation and excitement which was ready to explode into joy at birth, only to find it evaporating into sadness. Maternity hospitals can be extremely difficult places to be without a baby. Even in a quiet room of their own, bereaved mothers can hear newborn babies crying. Staff are unsure how to handle the situation and would feel more comfortable if the mother went home since they too feel they have failed.

Dads also can feel it's their fault. Although less involved in the pregnancy, they can feel guilty about not spending enough time with their wife or not being helpful enough. 'Why didn't I go with her to the scan?' 'Why didn't I insist she went to the doctor right away when she said things didn't feel right?' It also challenges the male ego not to have produced a healthy baby, somehow tarnishing pride and status. As hospital chaplain in a neo-natal ward, I often encountered fathers struggling to acknowledge that their tiny premature baby was about to die. Parents are surrounded by complicated machines, noises and bleeps. Watching the dials, the parents attempt to interpret their meaning and mentally 'will them to go up'. On top of this, the incubators make it very difficult to touch the child. All the equipment and tubes in the baby make the parents feel that the child belongs to the hospital and not to them. Suddenly, when the baby is dying, it's theirs. The machines are switched off and the baby placed in a tiny basket free of all wires and tubes. My role was to sit with parents in a quiet room as they held, perhaps for the first time, their dying baby. We would take pictures and absorb every second with the baby, right through death. However, often a father would struggle with holding the baby, and it would be common for him to dash out for fresh air to escape the pain of the situation.

Stillbirth

A stillbirth is when the baby dies before birth but has usually reached at least twenty-eight weeks of gestation. For parents it is the time when the beginning of life is the same as the end of life; when the time to live comes and the cry of the longed for baby becomes a sob of bereavement for the parents. Instead of anticipated baptism there is a sombre funeral.

For months parents have been preparing the home for the arrival of a new family member. A growing attachment has begun between mum and dad as they feel and see the movements of the baby in the womb. Every moment of the labour process is recalled as they rush to hospital when contractions start. From one minute to the next, all their hopes and dreams are turned upside down. Thoughts of telling relatives what has happened, contacting funeral directors and registering a death replace all their hopes.

'I just couldn't believe what was happening. All was going well and then suddenly there was a panic. Moments later I was holding my ill son, but fifteen minutes on he was dead. I couldn't believe the nurse was taking photos.'

When the mother has had a caesarean section under anaesthetic, the situation is further complicated, with a drowsy mother recovering from a major operation and wanting her baby. The possible reasons for such a death again play heavily on the minds of the parents. The short journey a baby makes through the birth canal from the warm womb into the cold outside can be the most hazardous of all journeys. There are many reasons why the journey can be unsuccessful.

The thought of the autopsy can be extremely stressful to the parents who want their almost perfect baby untouched. However, the pathologist is most skilful at hiding any autopsy incisions, and the knowledge it provides can compensate in the long run, calming parents about the reasons why their child died, and giving them hope for any future children. If genetic reasons are given for the death, parents have to face the statistics of whether such a death is likely to recur if they try again.

There comes a point when the mother has to leave the hospital for home. The feeling of walking out without your baby is a hollow one, but walking into an empty home is worse. The decision for the father of whether to move the cot, pram and nappies is a difficult one.

'As soon as I got home I went and washed the pram and cot thoroughly and then put them in the loft.'

The husband is often lost for what to do. Some mothers prefer to have baby things around a lot longer, holding on to their hopes. There are no nappies to change, or baby clothes to go and buy. Talking to relatives is difficult too, for they haven't seen the baby and find it hard therefore to talk about him or her. The mum has to cope not only emotionally but also physically, perhaps with stitches in her uterus and pain in her breasts from the production of milk. There is also the problem of what to tell other children.

Questions children ask are wide ranging:

- Where is my brother now?

- Can I see him?

- Will he ever grow?

- How can he breathe under ground?

- Will he ever have toys?

- Is it my fault?

How do you explain to a young child that their baby brother or sister is not coming home?

For some parents there is the sad reality that they may experience two or three miscarriages and stillbirths before they bring home a healthy baby. They have the difficult decision of whether to continue trying or to give up and be left only with a few photographs. Parents end up with so little to hold on to as time goes by.

'You go through so much and it's all for nothing; it makes me feel so annoyed. Pregnancy is all we have of our memories.'

'When I became pregnant again I felt disloyal to my dead child.'

Many parents end up bearing their loss silently, never referring to the painful events again. As hospital chaplain, I found that many parents would open up and talk about a previous miscarriage or stillbirth in a way they were unable to cope with in society outside the hospital. Expecting the birth of another baby brings back all their memories, fears and hopes.

Cot Death

Peter and Lynne were on holiday for the first time since the birth of their second child. A typical family of four, they had gone to Cornwall to visit their parents. Their first child was a healthy girl three years old. The second child was a boy, only weeks old. He was a healthy baby, the pride and joy of his father. Baby Thomas was still at the stage of having four hourly feeds, but in the early hours of one morning, when mum realised she had not been wakened by crying, she went to investigate. All seemed fine, so Lynne left Thomas to sleep for an extra half hour. But half an hour later was too late. Baby Thomas had died of cot death syndrome. The ambulance driver tried to resuscitate the baby to no avail; the policeman enquired to see if death had occurred through natural means; and the parents were left with an empty carrycot and grieving grandparents. The events of that day are engraved forever upon their memories.

Such a death raises many imponderable questions for parents.

- ❤ Could the death have been prevented?
- ❤ Why did the police come?
- ❤ Was it the parents' fault?
- ❤ Why is there no known cause?
- ❤ Can we believe all that we read about cot death?
- ❤ Should we have more children?

Since the cause of cot death is still the subject of endless studies, reports and media attention, there is a persistent feeling in parents that they may well have caused the child's death. Unable to say why their child died, parents are continually thinking through the tragic events and searching for a reason. The sudden death of an apparently healthy baby is so unbelievable, so shocking, that parents dumbfounded. Sudden Infant Death Syndrome (SIDS) is baffling, for it strikes with no warning. The baby that is fulfilling all the normal expectations of a parent may suddenly be found dead when mum goes to feed it. It may happen during the night or in the day time, in the parents' home or at a friend's. One baby was being taken in a carry cot in a car to the babysitter's home and in that ten-minute journey the baby stopped breathing.

Unlike miscarriage or stillbirth situations, the baby has been at home for a while. During this time the mother and father, as well as other members of the family, have formed strong bonds of attachment to the child. They have not only performed the basic parental duties – feeding, cleaning and protecting – but have watched the baby develop its own character, forming a unique personality. On discovering the baby, there is a natural tendency not to believe he or she has died.

'I'd never tried to resuscitate anyone, let alone my own baby. I just kept going until the ambulance arrived. I could hear my wife shouting to stop, but I couldn't. I was frightened of hurting my baby's chest but I thought what's a few broken ribs if he's alive.'

'It was awful. One moment my baby was dead and the next a policeman was trying to find out if I'd murdered him. They took the cot and mattress away; we didn't even have time to say good-bye.'

It is traumatic enough to know your beautiful baby will need a post mortem, but when there is no cause for the death it sets in motion a never-ending search for the reason why. Once physical illness is ruled out it is understandable that parents blame themselves.

- ❤ Was the baby too hot in the cardigan knitted by Grandma?
- ❤ Was the baby too cold?
- ❤ Had we started to feed him too early on solids?
- ❤ Did I pass on my 'flu to him?
- ❤ Was it our smoking, or our dog or cat?
- ❤ Did he not feel loved enough?

Parents rerun the events of the moments before discovering the baby dead over and over, searching for a reason.

Every few months, research into the cause of SIDS, leads to national or local publicity suggesting why it occurs. This in itself creates further guilt in the parents. If sleeping a baby on its front plays a part, all the parents who lovingly placed their child that way to prevent choking from sickness will feel they could have prevented the death.

'I feel angry at the medics who said it was okay to lay my baby on its tummy and to keep him especially warm.'

The fact that a coroner is involved only increases the feeling that someone must be to blame. The sense of guilt does not just stop at the parents. The ambulance attendants, nurses and doctors can feel inadequate. Grandparents can blame themselves, perhaps thinking it's genetic, and siblings can feel it was their fauld if they resented the intrusion of the new baby.

Later, there is the difficult decision of whether to have another child. During the pregnancy months, parents have to decide whether to seek help to calm their fears after the baby is born by using pulse monitors and weighing the baby frequently. For some parents this is a great comfort, whereas for others it only heightens their fears.

At whatever age a baby dies, parents never forget the specialness of the child. However, as the years go by they inevitably carry their memories alone.

'So few people knew my baby, but with older children others can share your memories.'

Many feel a sense of injustice as they hear of baby battering or anger at mums who go out to work and leaving their baby with a nanny.

'I feel as if I've lost my luck. I'm more morbid and bitter, things happen to me now, not to other people.'

Whether through a miscarriage, stillbirth or cot death, the loss of a baby leaves parents with scars which remain extremely painful for years.

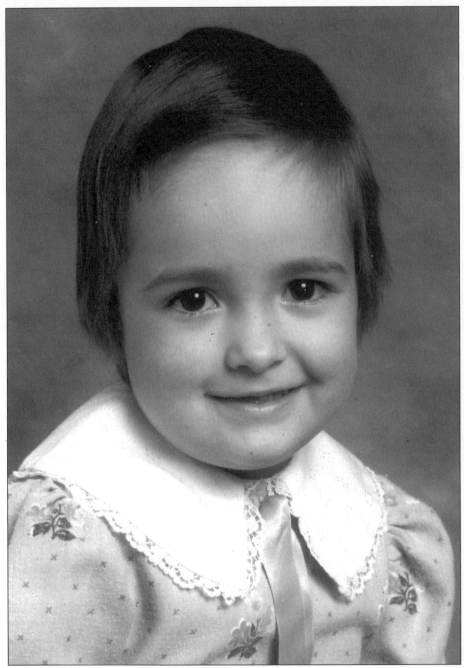

Kara, age 4, while she was fighting leukaemia.

3

Childhood Deaths

Oh call my brother back to me,

I cannot play alone.

The summer comes with flower and bee,

Where is my brother gone?

Felicia Dorothea Hemans

Life had not been easy for Margaret since her husband left her with two children, Carol, who was thirteen, and Simon, seven, although there were fewer arguments for the children to hear. However, after only six months Margaret had an even bigger problem to face. Her daughter had been complaining of backache for some time so they decided to see the doctor. At first the pain was diagnosed as being caused by a virus, but finally it was discovered that Carol had a brain tumour. After a five-and-a-half hour operation, the doctors were unsuccessful in removing the tumour. Carol was expected to live for only a few months. However, her mother would not give up hope and went on a search to find a cure for her daughter.

'I felt so resentful towards the doctors who didn't know of any new drugs to give her.'

During those difficult months, her husband applied to the court for custody of his son, Simon. Margaret did not know which way to turn. She was still hopeful when Carol came home with her oxygen cylinder. A Marie Curie nurse came each day to help.

'I never told my daughter as I wanted her to think she was getting better.'

The night Carol died her mother sensed a presence in the room which gave her strength.

> *'I'm not a religious woman, but I just knew Carol was going to die that night. I suddenly felt at peace. Carol had matured so much during those weeks. It was as if she had an old head on her shoulders.'*

At first Margaret had a sharp pain within, but gradually over the months after Carol died the pain became a deep ache. She still feels this ache eight years later. Margaret describes the first year of her loss as one in which she hid in the house, apart from going to the cemetery each day. The second year she read every religious book she could get her hands on. Five years later, Margaret was still on anti-depressants, still hoping that each year she would feel better. Meanwhile, her ex-husband threw himself into his work. He felt extremely guilty for not being around to support his daughter, and now felt trapped with no one to talk to.

By the timea child starts going to school, the mother has usually formed an incredibly strong bond with it, often stronger than the bond between husband and wife. Family life can revolve around attending the children, making meals, washing, ironing, transporting them to various activities. The parents' aim is to provide the very best for their child. Therefore, when parents discover they have a terminally ill child on their hands, it's as if life itself has stopped.

> *'Suddenly nothing in the world seemed important except the care of our child.'*

> *'How we got home from hospital I just don't know, we were in total shock.'*

> *'It is not only the emotional pain you feel but actual physical pain, which is excruciating.'*

> *'It was like watching a piece of paper with all your hopes and plans on it suddenly go up in smoke.'*

When a child dies suddenly there is no time to prepare for the loss. However, when illness is diagnosed, the family have the task of changing direction as they focus inward towards the child. In a sense, the terminally ill child becomes special as it receives not only the extra attention of parents but also of relatives and of the medical profession. As Knapp put it, 'this modification of parental and family activities must occur, because in the normal world activities are geared to the future.' [10]

Suddenly, only the day at hand is important. At first, parents of a child diagnosed as terminally ill react in a very similar way to parents who have suddenly lost a child. Shock and disbelief, accompanied by moments of anger and hostility are common.

> *'You are just not prepared for a doctor to tell you your child is terminally ill.'*

---

[10]R Knapp, *Beyond Endurance, op cit.*

It can take days for the diagnosis to sink in. Indeed, some parents simply will not accept the diagnosis. The thought of their precious child dying is too much to bear. Whether or not parents acknowledge the facts, there begins the search for a cure both by the medical profession and the parents.

Parents often begin to question, analyse and search for information. They grope for anything that will help them understand what is happening both to their child and themselves. This is probably a good thing as this positive attitude is passed on to the child indirectly, and gives the family the confidence to continue.

One of the difficult problems parents may have is knowing their child is terminally ill yet showing no visible symptoms. Also, as the prescribed drugs and treatment take effect, any sign of progress is seen as hope that all will yet be well. For the children who enter remission, although joy and relief is experienced, the sword of Damocles still hangs over the family.[11] A remission is the parents' dream, but even when it does occur there is the ongoing fear that the illness will return.

A dying child is not only sensitive to what message the parents convey but also picks up the 'vibes' that are given off by family, hospital staff and other patients. It is important to help the dying child itself to go through the grieving process, and if the parents experience early grief they may find it easier to face the inevitable.

During the difficult process of accepting the loss of a child, some parents are able to find comfort in the positive accomplishments their children contributed while they were living, and pride in their last achievements.[12]

. . . even the achievement of facing death. All the parents I interviewed whose children suffered in illness before death conveyed their pride in the courage of their child in the face of such suffering.

Terminally ill children themselves not only assess that they are dying but enter a bereavement process, ultimately coming to terms with their own death.[13] This developing knowledge of their impending death contributes partly to the rapid maturing of terminally sick children. It can lead to a change of roles in a family. Many parents begin to allow the sick child to control large sections of their lives. They begin to listen to the child as if he or she were an adult. Large portions of time are spent focusing on the child, at the expense of other children. This can cause resentment in siblings, later leading to guilt when they lose their brother or sister. Parents can ease the situation by explaining to their other children why they are behaving in a way that seems so unfair, and making a real effort to create a regular opportunity for the children to discuss their own feelings.

---

[11]G P Koocher and J E O'Malley, *The Damocles Syndrome*, McGraw Hill, London, 1981.

[12]ibid.

[13]E Kübler-Ross, *On Death and Dying*, Tavistock, London, 1970.

It is common for parents to seek some kind of miraculous recovery. This may lead to a long search for alternative treatment to what the hospital offers. Changing the diet, seeking herbal cures, religious intervention, may all play a part as the weeks progress. Although these may not prevent death, they give purpose, direction and hope. Most parents acknowledge that the greatest pain and stress is at the beginning of the ordeal and then nearer the end, rather than the end itself. During the ordeal, parents can feel guilty and ashamed. Could this be as a result of bad parenting? Is it a form of punishment? There is also the guilt of seeing their child go through painful treatment which they know will not work.

As death approaches, parents are beginning to think far more about the quality of day-to-day life the child has rather than on ultimate care. Subconsciously, parents may begin to distance themselves from the inevitable; they reach a stage of acknowledging that death is close.

4

Teenagers

Why should we want to see them again?

Because we love them.

Where did we get the capacity to love?

Surely it was the gift of God.

How could God foster within our

hearts the capacity to love,

letting it grow stronger

and more perfect with the years,

if at the end He meant to destroy it by death?

That would be futile, cruel and unthinkable.

He gave me the gift of loving.

He will give me again my beloved.

Leslie Church

Sally was the boss of the family. She had just celebrated her seventeenth birthday with an enormous party. The home had been full of excited teenagers bursting with energy. Sally was the sort of girl that always had friends around her. She was doing well at school with her 'A' levels . . . the sort of girl that set a good example in school. That's not to say everything was plain sailing in her life. Her strong-willed character created a few frictions in her home with her parents, John and Mary. Sally had got herself hooked on diets. As soon as she finished one diet, she would start another. Not far from the edge of anorexia, if it hadn't been for the support of her parents and Sally's determination, she might well not have recovered. But now her confidence was restored and she was back to the usual tussles with her older brother and disagreements with mum and dad. The main argument one weekend was her boyfriend. Dad was not keen on him, which only pushed Sally closer to Ian. Mum would encourage Sally to spend time with her in the kitchen baking cakes as an opportunity to get underneath this fiery character and find out what Sally really felt.

One night after Sally had been to school and finished her part-time job, her boyfriend rang, wanting to take her out with her friend. Dad immediately said no, but Mum – feeling Sally was under pressure – said yes, provided it was for a quick hour. As they left in the boyfriend's car, the atmosphere was tense between mum and dad. Several hours passed and Sally still hadn't returned home. The parents went to bed, but were only half sleeping when Mum suddenly woke with a start. She hesitantly went into Sally's secret domain, her bedroom, and for the first time ever opened her diary to find telephone numbers of her friends to ring. No one seemed to know where Sally had got to. Minutes later the police arrived. The three teenagers had given a lift to a friend and were on their way home,when their car collided head-on with a taxi which was on the wrong side of the road. Three people, including Sally, were killed. The boyfriend and the taxi driver survived. Sally's father had to go and identify her body at hospital.

The next few days were traumatic with many relatives, school teachers, and friends, especially Sally's friends, visiting the home. At times mum was calming Sally's friends down rather than the reverse. It was all so trying. It was difficult to patch together Sally's last few hours of life. Sally's parents found it hard to talk to Ian's parents. They wanted to know whether it was Ian's fault or his car. But Ian was recovering in intensive care so all that had to wait.

It was a small town but the church was overflowing for the funeral. Everyone seemed to want to share in the parents' grief. However, as time went by, they found themselves feeling isolated. Several friends kept away altogether after the funeral. It was as if Sally had never existed. Friends would ask after the son, but not mention Sally's name, while others would come out with painful comments, which Mary vividly reacalled:

> *'They'd tell me about the accident they had, or encourage me to let my daughter go, as if I could forget her. One friend suggested that her divorce had been much worse!'*

Sally's grandparents and relatives too found it difficult. John's father had been ill before Sally's death; once his granddaughter had died he seemed to give up the fight. Mary's brother lived in the north of Scotland so didn't come to the funeral and this created tense feelings in the family. Nevertheless, good things did result. Sally's father John recalled how he had lost his sister in a car accident when he was a child, and now began to understand better his parents' reaction over the years. Sally's grandmother suddenly started to visit her daughter's grave and began to talk about the her in a new way. Amazingly, the grandmother had also lost her sister in a bicycle accident as a child. Some of Sally's friends would visit and share with the parents stories about their daughter they had never heard. It was a great comfort to Sally's mother to know what a fine girl their daughter had been. Soon the family acquired a cat; Sally had always wanted one. Around the lounge were pictures of Sally at her best.

Five years have now passed, and Sally's brother is living away from home. He found life with his grieving parents rather claustrophobic. John and Mary have gone through ups and downs in their marriage, but they are still together. Work is far less important to them now. They have a simple attitude of living day by day. The contact with Sally's friends has dwindled down, which saddens them. They still feel a strong sense of anger:

♥ At the taxi driver who fell asleep at the wheel

♥ At the boyfriend

♥ At God

♥ At Sally

♥ At themselves for all the mistakes they feel they made

'The most upsetting thing is when people deny her reality; they think we're contagious so they keep away. We've lost not only growing up with her, her exams, marriage, children, but most of all we've lost a friend, our best friend who influenced us for good.'

Sally's story is typical of the events that follow the tragic loss of a teenager. To appreciate fully the impact of such a loss, we need to understand the intense and complex relationship that has been forged between parent and child. By the time a boy or girl is 14, their parents have invested thousands of hours in time caring for them. However, entering adolescence is a time of radical change both for parents and their children. Teenagers are people in transition. They are neither children, who need constant supervision, nor adults who are ready to take on the full responsibilities of life. They are somewhere in the middle.

This adolescence is an in-between time. It is like a bridge, spanning on the one side, the world of make believe and playtime, and on the other side, the world of bank accounts and trying to earn a living.[14]

As teenagers go through this transition, they can cause their parents not only moments of intense pleasure and joy but also great heartache. Teenagers are going through a time of physical change as their bodies take on the strength and fertility of a man's or woman's body. Such changes in a world where appearance is important can cause emotional and psychological strain. At the same time, their bodies are going through the sexual changes of puberty. This leads to a search for personal identity which, previously, parents provided.

As boys or girls become men or women there is that search within to find themselves. So many outer influences affect them as they discover who they are and who they want to be. TV, videos, magazines, all give out various messages to the young. For many teenagers pop music is not just a form of fun and entertainment but also conveys a message with which they can identify along with many other young people.

In the light of this, teenagers' relationships with their parents are changing. In the past, parents were their role models. Now children are forming their own attitudes, which may well differ from their parents and thus cause a clash of interests, attitudes and behaviour. It is therefore understandable that some parents to find the teenage years extremely trying. Although parents may feel they know their teenage children well, they can never know with certainty what they are thinking:

---

[14]R Hurding, *Understanding Adolescence*, Hodder & Stoughton, London, 1989.

- ❤ Will they pass exams?
- ❤ Will they ever get a job?
- ❤ How will they cope with leaving home?
- ❤ Will their parents ever get divorced?
- ❤ Are they capable of having sex?
- ❤ Should they masturbate?

Such thoughts and questions are in the young person's mind, locked away from their parents. The teenager is now controlling his or her own time, finance and relationships, with little input from parents. Such changes can lead to arguments with parents about untidy bedrooms, dirty clothes, dislike of friends and pressures of debt and drugs.

However, there are also moments of great joy. The fact that teenagers are usually full of energy tends to bring colour and life to any home. They provide a fresh insight for parents into the modern way of life. There are also the joys of seeing children achieve success with their varying abilities, and the closeness some parents develop in supporting them through the difficult times of exams. Teenage friends calling at the home can also bring enjoyable discussion as well as introductions to the friends' parents. Ultimately, there is the pleasure of becoming friends with your child, in a more equal relationship as they shape your life as much as you shape theirs.

In the midst of these complex parent-adolescent relationships, the loss of a teenager can leave a parent totally vulnerable. Death rarely arrives at the door when we are ready for it. It is understandable to find parents in a state of shock, having had a difficult relationship with a teenager, or following an argument, to be told their child has just died. Guilt is a common factor in bereavement for parents of teenagers. Many told me of their regret at how often they said no to the child. Where illness precedes the death, there is an opportunity for some parents to clear the air with their child, an opportunity to apologise for the argument, and a chance to listen to their son's or daughter's side. There is also the chance to begin to come to terms with the future death of a child and to begin the grief process. Parents say that it was extremely painful to sit at the side of a son or daughter in a coma, but months and years later found it a comfort to know they had been with their child at the end, fulfilling a parent's role of caring.

Afterwards . . .

When a teenager dies there is usually a high level of initial sympathy and support. Apart from the parents' relatives and friends, there are also the teenager's friends plus their parents, and teachers from the school or college. Parents begin a journey of discovery as they find out facts, events and talents relating to their child.

'I didn't realise how clever he was until afterwards.'

The bedroom of the dead teenager too can be a source of more information as parents have the opportunity of reading diaries. For many parents, the bedroom of their teenage child is a source of some comfort. Here, the senses of sight, smell and touch draw them close to their child.

Some parents begin to sleep in the child's room and eventually move into it altogether.

Funerals of teenagers are usually standing-room-only occasions as the church is filled with their contemporaries. For many, this will be their first experience of a funeral. (See Chapter Eight.) After the funeral, parents of the teenager's friends often keep their distance, as if death might be contagious.

'My son was taken to school for years by his friend's parents. Yet from the moment of his death they have not spoken to us.' (A parent after three years of bereavement)

Some of the dead teenager's friends may continue to call, which parents appreciate as it maintains the link with their child. Stories are shared, which bring laughter and tears. Parents learn a great deal about their son or daughter that previously they didn't know:

'We found out more about our daughter's school life from her friends than we knew before.'

'All sorts of stories have emerged from his friends, which are a comfort to us.'

However, as these young people get on with their lives, parents feel the pain of seeing them – and not their own child – go to college, graduate, marry and have children.

The care of the remaining children can bring tension – do parents loosen their control over other children or tighten it for safety? When couples are already split up or divorced, the distant parent can carry considerable guilt, perhaps feeling a failure at parenting.

When a child has become a teenager, parents have usually reached the age when it is too late to give birth to another child. When a teenager dies this reality is therefore magnified. Nothing can replace the son or daughter and life lacks any other focal point so the parents tend to ruminate upon the child.

'I think about him daily, in fact more so now he's dead than when he was alive. You don't need to think about them if they are alive.'

'I think nicer thoughts about her now she's dead than when she was alive.'

'I can't rebuild my life now, I'm too old to have children.'

The loss of a 'problematic' teenager leads to prolonged pain. It affects the parents' motivation at work: suddenly, all incentive to succeed seems so shallow. It also affects the social life of the parents whose friends are likely to be contemporaries who have children of similar ages. At social occasions, conversation tends to revolve around the children – their boyfriends or girlfriends, exam results, how they are getting on in their hobbies, etc. This leaves the bereaved parents more inclined to stay at home.

'Any social event we went to, we made sure from the beginning we had an escape route if we needed it. In the first three years I don't think we saw any event right through to the end.'

In the end, parents are left with the ongoing ache of 'shadow grief': life can never be the same again.

Ian, who was 28 when he was killed by a car while cycling to work.

5

Young Adults

Were a star quenched on high,
For ages would its light,
Still travelling downwards from the sky
Shine on our mortal night.
So, when a good man dies,
For years beyond our ken
The light he leaves behind him
Shines upon the paths of men.

Anonymous

Fred and Violet were a typical couple with two children. Alice was sixteen and still at school and Alan was twenty and studying theology at university. Alan was deaf in one ear and he coped with this admirably. He was a tall, handsome, blonde-haired young man with a marvellous future ahead of him. Term had just finished for Alan so he was on his way home for the summer holidays.

As Alan stood on the platform at the railway station, he didn't hear the train coming as it rushed through the station. He was standing too near the edge and the train caught his side. His parents reached the hospital only moments after Alan had died. His face was unmarked by the accident as Fred and Violet sat with him holding his still-warm hand.

Fred and Violet were not new to bereavement. They had both lost brothers in the war and their grandparents were dead. Their parents were devastated. Alan was the same age as the uncle he was named after, who had died in the war.

The events of the following days were a blur to Violet, except she could remember how beautiful and at peace Alan looked in hospital. Her parents came and took over all the necessary arrangements. Violet resented this intrusion. Life was a strain as she and Fred tried continue.

> *'For the first three years if I saw a tall blond person I would look intensely to see if it could be Alan.'*

> *'It all seemed false somehow, rather like living in a bubble. I was not suicidal, but I was extremely angry with God. But because Alan had faith, somehow my faith grew.'*

Some of their friends were helpful, but most didn't have a clue what it was like. One even asked Violet to watch a film about a train! Violet ended up in hospital with a minor problem, but eventually they came to terms with their loss, although they never got over it.

Alan's sister Alice felt neglected in the months afterwards. She had been especially close to Alan, remembering him by playing his tapes over and over again, but she never talked about him. Alice had always wanted to study medicine but suddenly changed her mind. Eventually she changed her mind again and became an excellent doctor. She fell for a handsome man, just like Alan, and the happily married couple had a baby boy. But then Alice suffered for nine years with cancer before she died.

Once again, Fred and Violet had nothing to organise as their son-in-law dealt with all the arrangements. Alice's husband wanted a quiet funeral; afterwards he kept himself and his son away from the grandparents. Fred and Violet had been given no possessions of Alice, nothing to remember her by. For Alan, Violet could picture how peaceful he looked, but Alice had fought such a battle that Violet could only recall an awful sight.

Fred and Violet are older and feel they have nothing left. They rarely see their grandson, and with so much time on their hands find it hard not to dwell on the past. The deaths have created a sort of distance in their marriage, a constant strain between them. Not long after Alice's death, Violet found herself once again in hospital.

> *'I was in shock for a long time after Alan died, whereas for Alice I knew it was coming, although it affected me just as deeply. I feel guilty I never spoke to Alice about dying. The only thing I have left now is Alan's ring.'*

We might well think that losing a child in its twenties would leave fewer scars than the death of a young child or teenager. However, from the view of an ageing parent such a loss is catastrophic. Perhaps the big difference, compared to the death of a younger child, is that the parents are not the legal next of kin. The wife or husband is the main mourner and is responsible for the funeral. Parents who have invested years of interest and energy in their child may find they are not consulted in dealing with its body or belongings. This can create a feeling of resentment, especially when parents believe they know their child better than any one else does.

All parents expect to die before their children. They may have already prepared their will, leaving their son or daughter as the executor and inheritor. When the tables are turned and young adults die, parents can feel cheated. They may now end up inheriting money and property from their child at a time of life when they least require it. The result is a sense of guilt, for still being alive, and because they have gained materially as a result of their child's death. Some parents take the positive step of giving away that inheritance to a relative or charity.

There is a deep wish within parents to be with their child - and may contemplate suicide. A milder feeling is loss of interest in life and society around them. It is easy for them to feel that they are being punished at a late stage of life. Indeed, this can lead to anger towards their child for dying and spoiling their plans.

'I felt so angry at my son's death, he should have known better!'

There are other characteristics specific to losing a child later in life. Parents have less information at hand about the life of their grown-up son or daughter. It is not easy to find out from your child's acquaintances and friends, as generally parents have not met or had any contact with them. Whereas with teenagers there is more of a link with school friends, with older children the social contact is scattered.

Another complication when a married child dies is that parents suppress their grief. It is natural for them to attempt to suppress their own grief so as to care for their son- or daughter-in-law and grandchildren. However, such suppression eventually catches up with parents. One or two years later, while parents are feeling the full impact of their loss, he bereaved in-law may have found a new partner and want to start afresh. Such a situation can be extremely painful, especially it if leads to grandparents not seeing their grandchildren.

'His wife has taken the baby away so we can't see him. I hate her.'

Some people end up assuming the role of parents to their grandchildren. This requires the grandparents to revert to the roles, habits, schedules and goals that they had in younger years at a time when they are hoping to take life easier. As much as grandparents may be willing to fulfil this role, it can lead to great stress, physically, mentally, emotionally and financially. In one case grandparents had acted as support parents to their son's children after he had lost his wife. Years later the son remarried, giving the grandparents the opportunity to have space for themselves in their retirement. However, nine months later their son's second wife died suddenly. The grandparents had to cope once again with bereavement, and to summon the physical energy required to support the grandchildren.

Older parents are at the stage of having to cope with their ageing and dying parents. The loss of a son or daughter intensifies the situation. At a time when life should be under control, parents suddenly find themselves out of control. As mature parents, they feel guilty for somehow not preventing the death . . . guilty for all the memories that come back to them of the difficulties and arguments they may have had with their child.

A mother who encouraged her son to leave home to find work at the coast said, 'I wished I'd not pushed him to get a job.' Only weeks later he died in a drowning accident.

Perhaps the greatest difficulty for parents losing an older child is the time they have spare to reflect. Younger parents have to keep going because of other children and their careers.

'At the very time I found space and peace in my life, suddenly that space and peace were totally shattered.'

Now there is only time to reflect on hopes lost and perhaps, eventually, to be able to look at the child's possessions and photographs with a sense of thanksgiving.

Section Two

Common Patterns in Grief

From the moment of conception, parents embark on a journey of discovery. The road is long, with many mountains to cross and several encounters with dark valleys: the experience of pregnancy, of a life force within you, moving, developing and growing daily; the all-encompassing experience of giving birth – involving excitement and anticipation along with intense pain and anxiety. In the first few months, there is a constant succession of peak experiences as the baby responds to your voice, begins to make noises and recognises you. The baby's first step is as thrilling for the parents as it is for the child. However, sandwiched between are moments of panic and worry. Nursing a child with earache or croup can be extremely worrying. There is also the gradual discovery that although your child loves you, he or she also wants to be free and independent. At first, there is a coming and going process as the toddler enjoys playing by himself, at the same time keeping an eye on mum and being able to get back into the security of her arms.

The start of school is a time when separation is more obvious, however painful it may be for young and old. As the child grows, the peaks and troughs continue. The joys of seeing your child building relationships with his contemporaries, learning to read and write, the pleasure of seeing a character and personality developing, and the child acquiring the skill to perform new activities. (At the very moment of writing this chapter, my middle child has just brought me the first cup of coffee he has ever made!) The low moments are the arguments and disagreements that develop between parent and child as the child seeks to assert his own opinions and will.

As teenagers, children still need to know they have their parents' support and a listening ear, but they also require a large degree of independence as they form their own life style. Tension can be close to the surface as parents grapple with the reality of losing their child to adulthood, when they still want to change and shape their child into their ways of thinking and behaving.

The tense relationship can settle down to one of mutual respect and friendship; young adults experiencing the freedom of independence yet still coming to parents who are willing to help with advice. For parents, there is the pleasure and satisfaction of seeing their hard efforts of parenting bearing fruit, and the hope that the family line will continue through their children. Death can strike at any time in this long journey, leaving the way ahead obstructed by pain and heartache.

Christopher, who had severe genetic problems, aged 18 months.

6

Bereavement and Feelings of Grief

I am standing on the sea shore.
A ship at my side spreads her white sails
to the morning breeze
and starts for the blue ocean.

She is an object of beauty and strength.
I stand and watch her until at last
she fades on the horizon.
Then someone at my side says,
'There, she has gone!'

Gone where? Gone from my sight – that is all.
She is just as large in the mast, hull and spars
as she was when she left my side.
The diminished size and total loss of sight is in me and not in her,
and just at that moment when someone by my side says, 'she's gone,'
others take up the glad shout, 'Here she comes!'

And that is dying.

Bishop Brent
1862 – 1929

Events before the child's death

The events immediately before the death of a child influence how families cope with the months and years ahead. The loss of life may hit a family immediately after a time of great joy. There can be a no more joyful event than the birth of a baby, the relief and pleasure of holding your own precious son or daughter. Hours later, to find the baby not as healthy as expected leaves parents devastated.

For older children, death may strike on or after a holiday, or just after achieving success in school exams.

Sophie at 18 had just begun a promising career. She was only weeks into her job when she was killed in a car accident on the way to work.

Alan had been on tour abroad with a youth orchestra. He'd had a marvellous time. Afer returning home to his parents, the very next morning he was found dead in his sleep, the victim of an unusual infection.

The parents are left to pick up the pieces. Eventually – years later for some – they are able to focus on the good moments before death. For other families the events just before the death remain with them in a disturbing way. In some cases, problems already exist in the family, perhaps with a marriage breaking up just weeks or months before the child's death. For others it may be that the relationship with the child was difficult. Arguments with children can be common. When this occurs just before the child dies, it leaves relatives with an intense sense of guilt and regret. In some cases, a family may have recently experienced another bereavement – the loss of a grandparent or an aunt or uncle.

Anticipatory grief

When a child has an extensive period of illness, parents begin to fear the worst. Endless hospital visits for medical treatment can be exhausting. Parents and the child can feel as if they have been put into a liquidiser; everything is in turmoil. Although caring for a terminally ill baby or child can be a gruelling ordeal, there are positive aspects which assist relatives in their bereavement.

The process of anticipatory grief can assist the parents not only when the moment of death arrives but also later on. However, this can only be beneficial if the parent is able to face the impending death and does not deny its reality. From those interviewed, I found that parents who had the opportunity to adjust to the impending death of their child could talk about the period before death with some positiveness. This agrees with the findings of other grief analysts.

The mother of a three year old girl who had been ill for a year explained how she oscillated up and down in her emotions. Times of hope and faith were followed by days of despair. However, she described how the last few months of her daughter's life were a very special time which gave her an opportunity to care in an all embracing way, and this later comforted the mother. Sick children benefit from constant reassurance that they are loved and cared for.

Generally, when there is anticipatory grief, parents show less guilt or self-blame, little extreme emotional or stressful reaction at the time of death, less anger and fewer depressive symptoms. There is also a greater tendency to formulate some way of handling the event that makes it more real, with less likelihood of reacting with disbelief and shock. However, it is still a time of great shock. Suddenly, when a child is in hospital, all the 'experts' take over in such a way that parents can feel they have already lost their child.

Parents of children who were ill for long periods of time tended to cope better after the death than did parents whose children were ill for a shorter time.[15] Parents with less than six months' warning and parents with over eighteenth months' warning of the child's death adjusted more poorly than parents who had between six and eighteen months to prepare for the loss.[16]

Parents whose children have cancer for more than two years are at higher risk from negative marital changes and depressive symptoms than parents of children whose cancer lasted less than two years.[17] Generally, an illness before death can allow parents to begin to rally a support team around them. Perhaps they may call in a priest to baptise the child. Here there can be the beginning of pastoral support. Or they may begin to learn which friends will be able to cope with the situation and thus be a source of support to the family.

The moment of death

When the child dies, parents are thrown into utter darkness. Suddenly, the invisible cord that joins a parent and child is cut. From that very moment the child has entered a world of death and the unknown, while the others find themselves in a world that ticks on as if nothing has happened. As Knapp puts it, death is not 'giving up' but 'giving in' to the ultimate. [18]

Doctors can assist by giving parents a little help in recognising that death is close. It is not always easy to know exactly when death will occur, so the medical profession is right to be cautious. However, sometimes parents do need to know the truth. It is also a time when doctors can assure the parents that the child, with the proper medical support, will die peacefully without pain and suffering. Parents can worry needlessly, afraid to ask the professionals.

---

[15] J Spinetta, et al, 'Effective Parental Coping following the death of a child from cancer'. *Journal of Paediatric Psychology*, 1981, Vol 6 No 3

[16] T Rando, 'An Investigation of Grief and Adaptation in Parents whose children have died from cancer', *Journal of Paediatric Psychology*, 1983, Vol 8.

[17] J Payne et al, Psychosocial adjustment of families following the death of a child, in *The Child With Cancer*, C Thomas, Springfield, Illinois, 1980.

[18] Knapp, *op cit.*

The first reaction to the loss of a loved one may be a temporary state of shock from which the parents recuperate gradually. When their initial numbness wears off and they collect themselves again, they often respond with, 'No, it cannot be true!' Kübler-Ross suggests that in our 'unconscious minds' we are all immortal, it is almost inconceivable for us to acknowledge that we too have to face death.[19] However numb and shocked parents may be, those moments of discovery remain engraved on their memories.

'I can remember every minute of the first two hours after hearing of his death.' (A mother five years after the loss of her son.)

For some parents this is actually a moment of release as they see their child finally escape from further operations, drugs, pain and suffering.

'It was the first time I felt release since my child had become ill, twelve months previously. However, later I felt guilty because I felt like this.'

'For six weeks I sat with Paul, holding his hand while he was on the life support machine. I talked and talked to him, so that when it came to switching off the machine, I felt ready.'

When illness has been prolonged, parents usually have the opportunity to be with their child at the point of death. For some parents this is so painful they want to escape. However, most find it a comfort to be with their child in the final minutes.

'I felt I couldn't hold my baby, yet I also felt I had to. I was terrified of it.'

'I just sat and held the baby for an hour.'

Although most bereaved people display feelings of anger, envy and resentment at some time in the weeks ahead, in some cases parents may feel extremely angry at the time of death. The anger may surface or be suppressed, and can be directed against various situations and people. One parent felt angry at his deceased son who fell from a great height. The father thought he should have known better. Others can feel resentful towards the care staff around them.

'I was told not to talk about the death to other mums in the hospital.'

'A nurse gave me a glass of sherry, but it wasn't a celebration!'

'I had sat up for nights with my child. The doctor encouraged me to go and get some sleep as he felt my daughter would last for days. Two hours later she died! I felt so cross with the doctor.'

Angry parents are harder for the relatives and friends to cope with than those who wish to deny the child's death. Parents' anger flows out in all directions, almost at random, and is difficult to contain.

---

[19]Kübler-Ross, *op cit.*

It may be the first time a parent has lost a loved one, or seen a dead person, especially a child. Parents are just not prepared for the events that take place immediately after death:

- The nurse taking a photograph of a dead baby

- The doctor telling the parents the child needs a post mortem

- The police arriving after a cot death

- Telling the hospital about a donor card only to discover that the child's body cannot not be used

- Having to identify their child after a car crash

All of these situations can cause angry reactions in the parents. Slowly, the reality of death dawns and parents begin to say to themselves, 'Yes, it has happened, but why my child? Why me? Why now?'

The days following the death

One of the most prolific creators of loneliness and a sense of desolation is the natural grief that accompanies bereavement. After the death of a child, the world seems to stand still, and if anything moves, parents perceive it is not meant for them. In the early stages of this shattering experience, the sense of loss of the loved one is so all pervasive that the bereaved person cannot believe the sun will ever shine again.

It seems quite outside the bounds of possibility that one could ever again face life with any semblance of enjoyment. [20]

How can parents respond to the unexpected death of a child? During the first few days, as relatives and friends gather around, parents are in a daze. They may experience such a mixture of emotions, that words fail them. When they speak, questions come to the surface more than anything else.

- How can this be happening?

- How can I possibly cope?

- Is the future worth living for?

- Will we survive this?

- Why don't you help me?

---

[20] J Sanders, *Facing Loneliness*, Highland, Croborough, 1988.

Unfortunately, relatives and friends feel just as helpless as they try to adjust to their own strong emotions.

'One of our friends, from the moment of Carl's death, has never been able to speak his name.'

It is as if parents awake expecting a clear blue sky only to find that darkness prevails for them and their relatives and friends. It is while parents are in the thick of the fog that decisions have to be made. Trying to make decisions about the funeral when you are still trying to put together the events of the past days adds pressure and tension.

There is a saying which goes, 'You don't miss the water till the well runs dry.' This has a particular meaning for those who have suffered the loss of a son or daughter. The full contribution a person makes in this world can only rarely be known while he or she is still alive. We all seem to take for granted people who are very important to us. Our appreciation of the enrichment they produce in our lives, and their central place of importance in our world is just not fully realised. We cannot begin truly to miss these 'significant others' until they are gone from us. Countless parents have learned this agonising lesson following the deaths of their children.

The first few weeks of bereavement seem totally unreal for the parents. Several described those early days as 'walking around in a bubble'.

'Silent, swift, irreplaceable, the scythe has swept by, and we are left . . . The mail comes, the 'phone rings, Wednesday gives place to Thursday, and this week to next week. You have to keep getting up in the morning and comb your hair (for whom?), eating breakfast (remember to get out only one egg now), making the bed (who cares?). [21]

'It can seem 100 years ago and at other times like five minutes. I lost interest in everything except day-to-day necessities.'

Parents long to hear the child's voice, his laughter, or walk into his bedroom and see that bundle of sleepiness under a blanket, all rolled up, on the verge of waking up and saying, 'Morning, Mum.' There is still a ray of hope that somehow it has all been a nightmare from which they will wake and find their child alive and well.

'I kept expecting him to walk into the room or to receive a letter saying he was okay.'

Some may, in their minds, enter a form of bargaining with God, 'If only you make this a dream I'd wake up and be different.' But each day is the same grief-filled experience as the parents carry real physical pain within themselves.

There are times when parents think they have seen their son or daughter. Some report the vivid exprience of seeing their child's image or spirit – and widows also experience this phenomenon.

---

[21] J. Sanders, *op cit.*

Seeing another child with similar build and wearing clothes like their own child's can heighten the sense of search for the loved one. This inevitably leads to increased disappointment and heartache.

All around the grieving parents are reminders of their loss. The empty bedroom, clothes that still need washing, photographs, special food in the kitchen, and perhaps a pram or buggy. On top of this there is the characteristic smell associated with an individual, particularly a baby.

A mother who lost her baby in a tragic car accident couldn't sleep unless she went to bed holding the baby's Babygro. The special smell of the gown was a comfort. However, after a few weeks the mother washed it and has not stopped regretting it, for the characteristic smell was gone!

Each morning the post brings cards and letters of sympathy. It is common for other parents who have experienced the loss of a child to write offering support. These letters seem to be a tremendous help as they come from those who truly understand. Upsetting mail also arrives. The exam results which come just too late – or in one case a letter from the hospital offering a date for a heart operation with a message from the Consultant (who had cared for the boy from four months old to the age of seventeen) which said, 'Good luck in the exams'. The parents under-standably found this extremely upsetting. Another parent said, 'Weeks after my son's death, his 'A' level results arrived.' When older children have died some families have found they still receive mail years later.

However helpful the funeral director and clergyman may be, parents can also feel like they are intruding into a family affair. As friends and relatives come and go from the home, the family can feel in a state of limbo, between the death and the day of the funeral. One source of comfort is the flowers and the cards that the family receive. The kind words expressed in simple terms mean a great deal.

Other worries can also pervade the mind of the bereaved parents. There may be the worry, especially in young families, of the cost of the funeral. They wonder whether they should take sleeping tablets prescribed by the doctor. They wonder what they should do with all the child's possessions? In the case of suicide, there may be a search for a note from the child. All the time, the world continues to rush by as if nothing significant has take place. Little things become hard to do:

'I went to the dentist, but when he asked me how I was, I got upset. I had to leave half way through the treatment.'

Anger, despair and guilt may well up at any moment. A parent may even have a few good days, only to be engulfed with grief again. One parent scraped all the wallpaper off her walls, while another suddenly broke every plant pot in the house.

The first few months

The early months of loss seem to be a mixture of guilt, anger and fear, all constantly soaked in tears.

'I cried every night for six months,' said one mother after the suicide of her teenage son.

'I constantly cry, I'm afraid of stopping in fear of forgetting him. When I do stop crying I feel guilty for showing any signs of getting better. If I love him how can I possibly stop crying?'

When we think about the death of a child we are likely to conjure up an image of a death by illness in hospital or at home. We may be able to visualise more painful scenes, such as drowning, or a car accident. We seldom think of what proceeds from such unexpected deaths. The post mortem, an inquest and perhaps a trial. The whole process of law courts, inquests and a trial tend to confuse and delay the working out of the grief process. All the parents involved with inquests complained about how painful they found the procedure. It was common to find an inquest postponed at least once.

'I would get myself all worked up, my hands would be shaking, only to find it was postponed!'

One family went to the inquest four months after the death, along with school friends of the dead child who were in the car that crashed. At the inquest they found the driver who was involved in the crash there with his lawyer, whose questions put great pressure on the school children, for which they were totally unprepared. The parents said how angry they were at the lawyer who attempted to pass the blame on to people they saw as innocent!

The outcome of trials and inquests can lead to further heartbreak for families. Parents of a 26-year-old son killed when his bicycle was struck by a car from behind were horrified to find that the driver only got a fine of £45 and three penalty points.

The feelings and emotions expressed in the aftermath of such tragic losses are in no way abnormal reactions. Anger, hostility, helplessness, frustration and guilt, although very negative feelings, are nevertheless genuine emotions experienced by all who suffer losses of any type. Parents cannot get rid of these feelings and emotions by going through some of kind of counselling, yet they do need to be acknowledged and shared with those who care.

Many assume the bereaved should be getting on with their lives a few months after a death, but for most, the situation is getting worse, not better. Physical pain remains, along with the mental strain of constantly thinking about the lost child. The parents' lives are in a state of disorganisation, as other children, the home, work and friends are neglected. The impact on surviving children is immense, for they have not only lost a brother or sister but also – albeit temporarily – parents as they are absorbed in grief.

The home is a constant reminder of the child. Many parents find themselves sitting for hours in the child's bedroom surrounded by memories. A voice that sounds similar to the child's, a piece of music, or someone who looks similar can suddenly cause them to burst into tears. Some find they initially have to take down pictures of the child so as to control themselves, but gradually photographs became very important in recalling the loved one. In almost all the homes I visited, there were several photographs of the dead child. However, parents did not seem to find it easy to look back at video recordings.

Holding on to possessions

All around the home are the possessions of the loved child, which can either serve as a comfort or increase the pain. When young children die, it is the pram, the buggy or the cot. For teenage deaths, it tends to be their bedroom. Does a parent tidy it all away immediately or leave it for months – or years? On the whole, there seems to be a clear difference in reaction between the loss of babies compared to older children. In the majority of cases, where a baby has died in hospital and has spent no time or only weeks at home, parents seem to prefer to remove all signs of the baby at an early stage. Some packed all the baby's clothes and put them in the loft in the same afternoon the baby died. Several of the parents, mothers particularly, expressed regret at doing this. With hindsight, mothers feel they could have coped with the toys and clothes better if they had not put them away so soon.

The longer the child has lived at home, the longer it takes the family to remove his or her belongings. A person's bedroom portrays something special about them. The older the child, the more they have made the room their own. The decor and personal belongings give a feeling that the person is around. When it comes to the death of that person, relatives want to be as close to them as possible, and this is best achieved by being in the bedroom. Several families told how they would just sit in their child's bedroom taking in the smells and atmosphere that remained. In one case, a fiancé moved into his dead girlfriend's bedroom for several weeks to be as close to her as possible. Other families talked of sitting in the child's room to open the many condolences and cards sent to them. Suddenly, drawers kept secret and diaries not read could be opened and touched to explore closer the mind of the dead child. One mother would go into the bedroom and sniff at her son's clothes, yet was reluctant to invade his privacy by touching them

Most families that lost older children left their child's bedroom untouched for at least one year. Many had not altered the bedroom at all, even three to four years on. Others had changed the room, but because of some external reason. A few that changed things within weeks seemed to regret the decision. Because of this attachment to the room, several families described the difficulty of moving house and having to sort out the treasured area. One mother felt that sorting out her daughter's bedroom years later led to her having a nervous breakdown. Another couple felt so attached to the child's room that they eventually moved into it. Even pet animals seem to recognise the specialness of a son's or daughter's room: one family's dog would go and sit in the son's bedroom for a couple of hours each day.

Although many parents never redecorated their child's room, none felt it had become a shrine. It was simply a place of identification, a place of pain, but also of special memories not to be lost, a place where they could be alone with their thoughts, but also a place they could walk out of and get on with life. Others in the community do not seem to accept this as a natural desire. Several parents felt doctors and health visitors would have preferred them to alter the room and remove the possessions. A health visitor's comments made one mother feel guilty that she had not altered the room. However, she decided that deep within her she did not wish to change it.

Parents felt that people around them were afraid they would be too mournful and not face up to the situation. There is evidence that parents are afraid that they will somehow lose the memory of their child altogether. In this respect, the bedroom acts as a point of contact between the past and the future. Clothes and personal belongings can also play a part in comforting parents. Many parents found it helpful to wear a child's ring or crucifix, or to place a child's special possession in a prominent place.

I have come to the conclusion that parents can deal with the emptiness of the future produced by the death of a child only by filling those voids with images of the child they once had, through thoughts, memories, and open discussion. Only in this way does such a loss become a reality.[22]

Dreams

Dreams and premonitions are recurring theme when talking to parents who have experienced loss. Such vivid experiences may occur before death, at the moment of death or afterwards in grief. The majority of mothers, as opposed to fathers, were able to recall this experience. Only a handful of parents seemed to relate the death to some previous thought or experience.

One mother dreamed of her baby choking in the middle of the night. She rushed to the child to cuddle him. The mother often said to the child,' You mustn't die'. Then the child died of cot death syndrome at the babysitter's house. Another mother was busy teaching when she suddenly felt faint and had to sit down. Later she was told her teenage son had died in a car crash at the very time she felt unwell. Clearly, such experiences may be post-created subconsciously as a mechanism for accepting that the death was inevitable. However, those who experienced such incidents were convinced that they were real events.

The majority of parents could remember dreaming of their child after its death. They could recall the dreams with fond memories and saw them in a positive light. Parents reported that when they had dreamed of their child, they would awake feeling peaceful and refreshed. However, when they did not recall dreaming, then they were more likely to awake feeling exhausted. Parents'

---

[22]R. Knapp, *op cit.*

dreams were varied, but most saw them as positive events which had a healthy effect on the dreamer.

'When I dreamed of my daughter I felt better. I'd see her in a field with her favourite dress on. I'd say 'You're all better', and she would reply, 'I love you,' and then walk back.'

Some recalled always dreaming the same dream in the same location.

'It was as if it had a healing effect on me. It was not a familiar place, but each time I dreamed it I felt better.'

In one case, two teenagers had been in a car crash. One died instantly and the other was in intensive care. The mother of the survivor dreamed that she saw a field of primroses, and girls, including the dead child, were coming to take her son. She cried out, 'Please leave him' at which they turned and left. After this dream the boy began to recover. At the girl's funeral, a school friend read a poem about primroses. She could not possibly have known about the dream, and this gave great comfort to the parents of the girl who had died.

Dreams are not always positive. In a few cases parents would wake up crying because of a dream. But in the majority of cases parents were glad they had dreamed and wished they had continued. Most of the dreams took place during the first year of bereavement. Women seemed to dream more than men and this caused tension in some relationships. Several men said they wanted to remember dreams about their child and felt envious of their wives because of their closeness to the child through the dream. Although the dreaming experience was short lived, in most cases parents said, even years later, how the dreams were still vivid and a comfort to them.

The first years

The first year of bereavement brings to the surface both the change of routine in life and the recollection of all that took place over the previous year. For those who have lost younger children it is the radical change from taking their children to school, meeting the same parents each week, the regular lifts to music lessons or youth groups. Parents experienced considerable pain as they watched other parents still carrying out the role they used to play and this continues for years. Parents sometimes bump into former classmates of their child which makes them imagine what he or she would be like now, compared to the memories which are fixed in time.

It is not only the normal healthy routine of life that parents miss but also the regular times of visiting hospital for treatment.

'We went to hospital every Tuesday for four years with our daughter. It left an enormous gap; in illness we at least had a routine. We chose a Tuesday for the funeral.'

Some parents may have to cope with never getting away from the scene of death - children sometimes die at home, through illness or accident. One mother had to drive to work each morning past the spot where her daughter had been killed in a car accident.

It is common for parents to go through their minds and recall exactly what they were doing with the child this time last year. Birthdays, Christmas, holidays and the anniversary of illness and death are the worst times. Parents seem to brace themselves weeks in advance for these dates to arrive, often finding that the fear before the anniversary is actually worse than the day itself.

'I had mixed reactions at Christmas because my son enjoyed it so much, yet it could never be the same without him.'

'I hate birthday parties and holidays. They are the very time when the person who would love it most is missing.'

Another mother decided to look at Christmas and birthdays positively by buying presents for her dead son.

'It was my way of acknowledging him. If I bought first of all for him I could then allow myself the freedom to buy for the rest of the family.'

However, most mothers said they felt guilty at these events and would have preferred to miss them altogether. Christmas can be difficult because society all around is busily preparing for a celebration. Several parents said they had stood in a shopping centre wanting to shout out:

'How can you be busy buying, I've lost my son.'

Other parents found it hard to leave home for a holiday, feeling they betrayed their child by leaving it behind.

'For the past three years now we have always come back from holiday via the crematorium.'

Suicidal thoughts are common, particularly among parents who have lost an older child.

'I just wanted to die in the first year. Breast cancer, anything – just to be with my son.'

'I would lie in the bath and wonder whether I had the nerve to drown myself and end it all.'

'You can go for weeks and suddenly the events go round and round in your mind and before you know it you're getting depressed.'

In younger families, although the pain is still great, there may be the possibility of having another child. However, in older families all seems lost. Mothers especially feel there is no hope, no way of satisfying or fulfilling their lives, and no purpose in continuing without their deceased child. Thy also wish to escape the physical pain that they feel within. Fortunately, the vast majority of parents do not commit suicide, but it is an understandable reaction and reveals the depth of despair and depression they experience. The outcome is that parents don't fear their own death; they have a dull, fatalistic feeling that lingers for years.

By the end of the first year, parents think they must have experienced the worst: the loss of a child, difficult family relationships, lack of motivation, coping with people who make hurtful comments and even avoid them in the street. Surely, things will get better. However, many say the second year is worse than the first, because parents feel more removed from the events of the past. The first anniversary does not suddenly make things better. On top of this, people seem to have forgotten the dead child and never mention his or her name. They expect parents to be more sociable and back to their normal selves, but parents see it very differently. For them, the bubble of life has burst. Marriage and family life may be tense, the husband may be under pressure from his poor performance at work. The court case linked to the death may be behind them. There seems so little to look forward to. When other accidents and illnesses occur, which are similar to their dead child's, it jars the memory of parents. They are angry and disappointed the same type of accident happens, feeling that society has not learned the lessons of the past. Parents may also feel pangs of envy when they see other people survive accidents or illnesses similar to their child's.

Parents who have lost babies and young children have to decide whether to start again, and if they do, how to cope with their fears for the new child's future. Parents who have lost teenagers and older children have to cope with contemporaries getting jobs, degrees and even sending them wedding invitations. For a few, this period of loss is just too much, the fact of death is so all consuming, the bereaved are obsessed by it. The battle within gives way to breakdown and illness.

For others, the routine of work gets them through each day until they find themselves beginning to have at least some good days. However, all parents I've spoken to acknowledge thinking about their child every day.

'You begin to learn that you will have good and bad days, you can't predict which they will be, but at least you learn that, like the weather, there will be continual change.'

'I believe that just as clouds come and go so I have good and bad days. There is no logic to these days. I now at least know that if it's a bad day it will pass; this is the only way I can have any hope.'

'We talked a lot to each other and just expected everything to get better. After three years I realised it wouldn't. I had to just get on with life as it is.'

Five years on

The natural assumption in our society is that after a year or two a bereaved person should be back to normal, living life to the full. The thought of someone still struggling through life because of a death five or even ten years earlier will seem strange to many. Yet, from the parents I have interviewed, 54% said they had not come fully through bereavement after five years, and the figure was still as high as 20% after ten years. What is equally revealing is the number of parents who said they still had problems to resolve relating to the death. Here, approximately 60% of parents at both five years and ten years after bereavement said they still had problems.

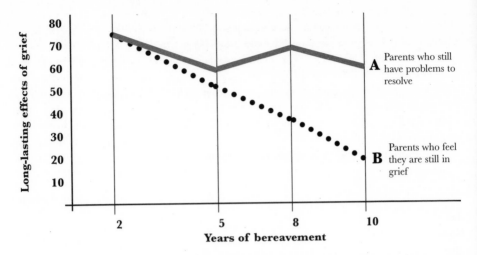

How can we account for these figures? We might expect a small percentage of parents still to have problems and be in delayed bereavement. However, these figures show that a greater number of parents than expected is still struggling after five or ten years.

I believe there are several factors playing a role in these parents' lives. Society has usually forgotten the events of ten years ago. People around the bereaved have either moved on or they are tired of discussing events which to them are past and gone. Parents will often hear the words, 'You need to put it behind you now and start afresh.' However, that's just what older parents cannot do – and no parents wish to do. One mother put it this way:

'They think I can press an 'erase' button and all my memories will be gone.'

We can, perhaps, forget minor things in our past, but when we have loved our child so deeply it is impossible to let go. Many parents make silent vows never to forget and hold on tightly to memories of their child. Therefore, the 'shadow grief' that remains is the cost of their love and commitment to the memory of their child. As time goes on, if memories get distant, parents feel guilty. By trying to get on with life, parents can push memories to the back of their minds, and when they surface they can seem muddled. This is a disturbing feeling as parents try equally hard to hold on to each remembered event clearly. It becomes increasingly difficult for parents to find people willing to listen five years on; they are unable to release their thoughts and so carry on this inner frustration.

If they have younger children, parents worry that they too may die at the same age as their deceased brother or sister. If they have older children, after five or ten years they may well have left home, creating a void in the parents' lives. It is common to find marriage problems continuing years later as the death of a child drives a wedge between the partners. As parents react differently to the death, over the years it can cause resentment between husband and wife.

Ten years on

As we endeavour to grasp what it must be like still grieving for a child ten years on, listen to how five parents now see their situation:

'If final acceptance is getting over it, then I never will! But if acceptance is missing him, then I am there now.'

'I still have off days, especially when I see mums with children the same age as my child.'

'When someone comes up to you and asks, "How's your daughter?" it's like a dagger turning in me.'

'I still avoid pregnant women.'

By now, parents have realised that although they may be coming to terms with their loss, they will never get over it. They continue to hold on to the picture they had of their child at death. Contemporaries have grown and changed, but parents find it difficult to imagine their child anything other than how he or she was the day they died.

When parents have lost older children who already had children of their own, there may now be the complexity of relating to grandchildren. The daughter- or son-in-law may have remarried and prefer the grandparents not to talk about the deceased. Yet the bereaved parents may be desperately wanting to share with their grandchildren what their father or mother was like.

It is important for bereaved parents to understand that their reactions and feelings are normal. It is normal to want just another five minutes with your child. It is normal to hold onto bad days just because you want to. It is normal to have photographs of your child always prominent. As one parent, after ten years, put it:

'I still feel resentful for the loss of my four-year-old. I don't go over it but still live with it. You can't put it behind you because it's all too precious!'

Andrew 18, on his scooter. He was killed in an accident unrelated to scooters.

7

Personal Relationships

One night I had a dream.
I dreamed I was walking along a beach with the Lord
and across the sky flashed scenes from my life.
For each scene I noticed two sets of footprints in the sand.
One belonged to me and the other to the Lord.
When the last scene of my life flashed before us,
I looked back at the footprints in the sand.
I noticed that many times along the path of my life
there was only one set of footprints.
I also noticed that it happened at the
very lowest and saddest times in my life.
This really bothered me and I questioned the Lord about it.
'Lord, You said that once I decided to follow you,
you would walk with me all the way.
But I have noticed that during the most
troublesome times in my life
there is only one set of footprints.
I don't understand why in times when I
needed you most you should leave me.'
The Lord replied, 'My precious child
I love you and I would never leave you
during your times of trial and suffering.
When you see only one set of footprints,
it was then that I carried you!

Author unknown

The urban family today is usually small, consisting of no more than one or two children. In times past, when families were larger, the loss of one child did not adversely affect the functioning of the family system. Infectious diseases took a heavy toll so child deaths were 'expected' and tolerated much as elderly deaths are today. Today, our few children represent our future and when they are terminally ill our future falls into jeopardy. When they die, we feel our future 'dies' with them.

Husband and wife

Grieving is a lonely process, so unless a family can draw upon sufficient resources to give it strength, it is truly put 'at risk' and stress from the death of a son or daughter may provoke a massive crisis. Sometimes, even the closest of couples find that they can provide each other with only limited support after loss. As much as they might wish to, the parents cannot 'make it go away' for each other. Their feelings can also never be exactly the same; each one grieves at a different pace and in a different way. In trying to cope with their own individual pain, parents have less strength for each other.

In the back of each of their minds, they believed they could lean on each other as they mourned. But you cannot lean on something bent double from its own burden.[23]

This realisation comes slowly to couples and, at a time when they expect the greatest closeness, it may lead to resentment and disappointment.

'Death puts a sort of distance between you in your marriage that creates a strain.'

In some cases, divorce had resulted after the loss of a son or daughter.

'Our marriage had cracks but our daughter cemented over them until she died. Our other child was hyperactive, so his father felt he had been left with the "booby prize".'

When interviewing couples where the marriage had been a success, there seemed a willingness to be extremely open about their marriages, even when both partners were present.

'We had a good marriage and a happy start. It is only because of this we feel we've come through such a bad patch.' (A mother who had lost two babies.)

Where the child has been ill before death, areas of conflict can arise which then sour the relationship.

'When my son was in hospital, I wanted to stay with him, but my husband, not liking hospitals, always wanted to come home. This created conflict and later I felt bitter and angry towards him.'

---

[23]H S Schiff, *The Bereaved Parent*, Crown Publishers, New York, 1977.

Often a husband has not been as involved in the early child rearing years and so may not be as close to the child, and thus reacts differently in bereavement. In general, women and men seem to grieve differently. Our culture assumes that after a family death the man will be steadfast and the immediate family will lean on him. People enquire how his wife is 'feeling' and 'taking it' or 'holding up'. At the same time, he is expected not to show his feelings. Men sensed this expectation of them at work. In the first few months, a man may be silent about his loss.

> *'My husband was not so close to my son so he reacted differently. It made us feel further apart. I felt bitter that he didn't care. My husband just didn't want to talk, whereas I couldn't stop referring to our child. This was a major factor in our divorce.'*

Local friends can be a tremendous help, simply by listening. However, wives expressed their regret that the one person they most wanted to talk to – their husband – didn't want to approach the subject.

Lack of communication is one of the major factors in the breakdown of relationships. This may verbal, not talking about the situation, or physical as the couple withdraw into themselves, or even avoid each other as they go their individual ways.

Ten years after a child had died of choking, its mother wanted to talk about it but her husband refused. (He also refused to be interviewed.) Several men said that they were pleased that their wife was being interviewed but declined themselves. They were, however, willing to fill in a questionnaire. Such a lack of communication raises extremely strong reactions, even if divorce does not result. A mother twelve years into bereavement said:

> *'My husband would not talk about the death of the baby. I felt hate for him because of it. Our marriage has never been the same.'*

The older the child, the more men were willing to talk. Where babies and very young children are concerned, although fathers feel the depth of pain as much as mothers, their contact with the child has usually been less. They have been less involved with feeding and nappy changing and so seem to have less to refer to. Nevertheless, just because men seem less able to articulate their feelings, it does not mean they do not feel intense grief. A man seemed more likely to bury himself in his work, go for a drive alone, or visit the cemetery without telling anyone.

One father was worried about sharing his emotions because his wife was delicate. He would instead go out and walk alone for hours. After two years, his suppressed emotions came to the surface and he ended up in hospital. Up to that point, his wife had thought he just didn't care!

Another father felt guilty that five years on he seemed to have fewer problems coping than his wife. Where there has been a breakdown in marriage before death, guilt seems to be high on the agenda. In one case, because the father was seeing his children less, when the daughter died he not only felt guilty but his other children stopped wanting to see him, thereby increasing his dilemma.

No couple believed that their marriage was especially stronger because of what they had come through. To survive together was an incredible achievement in itself. Where marriages seemed to have the fewest tensions there were signs of good communication, a willingness to listen and to support when one or the other was down, an agreement on activities, and manifest signs of affection each day.

Brothers and sisters

As parents cope with their own grief in the loss of a baby, child or young adult, they may also have to deal not only with marriage problems but also the disturbing reactions of surviving children. This may surface in a number of ways: poor health, emotional one-upmanship, competing for attention or withdrawal into reclusiveness.

A child's reaction to a death may not be obvious, especially if it is too young to talk about its feeling and the parents are in a state of shock themselves. Other children often say they felt they lost not only a brother or sister but also their parents. Many parents told me they were so consumed with their own problems of grief that they were unable to observe or cope with their other children's problems.

Obviously, a child's understanding of death varies depending on his or her age and parents have to take this into account when explaining to them what is happening. Books for various age groups are available, and these can help.

Although children were not specifically interviewed, many parents described how their other children reacted to loss. Several mentioned their regret at not allowing the children to go to the funeral service, thinking they were protecting them. The parents found later that the children resented not going. One teenager wanted to visit his dead brother at the Chapel of Rest but was discouraged from doing so because of the condition of the body. However, it prevented the boy from sharing fully in the pain of the parents which therefore made him feel excluded. In another family, a boy of twelve did not go to the funeral but regretted it because he felt he had let his dead sister down. Twelve years later he talked to his parents about this and wept. He felt much better afterwards.

Even young children said they would have preferred to go with their parents to a service rather than be left at home. Months after his brother died, a young boy saw an open grave and expressed his surprise. 'Is God a mole?' he asked, 'for God can't see my brother down there.'

Peer relationships are important at this stage; children benefit if they can identify with another child who has also experienced loss. There is a clear change of role when a child loses a brother or sister. In several homes where the eldest child had died, the next child made friends with the dead brother's or sister's friends. This seems to be both a comfort to the child, who is filling the void left by his brother or sister, and a help to the parents, who seem to benefit by still relating to the dead child's friends. However, parents did convey their regret that other children had matured more quickly because of the death. The parents had not only lost one child but felt they had lost the growing years of the other children.

One of the commonest experiences described by other children is feeling totally isolated in their grief when all the attention seemed to focus on the parents' loss. Parents themselves afterwards acknowledged with some regret that this took place. A teenager who had lost an older brother said to his parents, 'Why is it people come and talk to you about your loss but not to me?'

Parents have the tendency to send children out of the room when visitors come to talk specifically about bereavement, in an attempt to protect them. In reality, it only ostracises them further. It is understandable that parents misunderstand the needs of other children, for children can hide their true feelings most convincingly. A teenager in his need left a message in a drawer, where he knew it would be found, saying how much he missed his brother and how wretched he felt. Since many parents can find the teenage years a difficult period in any case, quiet, sulky behaviour can be just taken for granted. Over the first year, the conversations in the home can seem totally to revolve around the deceased. On top of this, the dead child's photograph is often prominent in the house, all of which increase the intensity of emotions for surviving children.

'My daughter seemed to take the loss in her stride. It was months later when I suddenly realised how sad she had become.'

In another family, one son wouldn't talk about his deceased brother at all, yet months later his mother saw him visiting the grave. Still later, his sister reacted by attempting suicide.

What must be acknowledged is that, just like parents, other children in the family react differently. One child might talk excessively about the deceased whereas another might close up like a clam. When a parent retreats, or withdraws silently for an extended period of time, the child survivor 'loses' that parent; moreover, the child interprets the parent's behaviour as a personal rejection. The parent may consciously deny the child's feelings in the hope that denial will help suppress sadness, longing and despair in the family. This only complicates the mourning, rather than making it easier.

Most commonly, siblings' reactions to death are fear, guilt, anger and confusion. They may have many fears:

- ♥ Fear of losing a parent
- ♥ Fear that they too will die
- ♥ Fear of going to sleep
- ♥ Fear of being separated from the family
- ♥ Fear of being unprotected
- ♥ Fear of sharing their feelings with others

When teenagers lose a brother or sister, they may identify very closely with that death, having feelings that range from vulnerability to complete helplessness. Other children are often afraid that they might die at the same age. Parents also experience this fear of losing another child in the same circumstances. This led many parents to describe how protective they had become of their surviving children.

> *'I was afraid to argue with my son, so I gave in to all his requests. You hesitate to disagree, provoke or argue, and you become more liberal because of fear of losing another.'*

With older children, this protection becomes frantic when they are ready to leave home. One son stayed at home longer than he would normally have done to be a comfort to his parents.

Younger children are more likely to worry and fret that their parents might die, whereas older teenagers can rationalise this, but fear more for themselves. When other deaths occur in the neighbourhood, it can trigger off suppressed fears. One youngster twitched and worried that his parents would die. A girl in his class lost her mother, and this increased the boy's anxiety. With younger children too, cot deaths can be especially frightening. When death occurs for no apparent rational reason, it leaves children with little justification for the tragedy.

> *'Why did he die, mummy? He wasn't ill.'*

In the same way as this may console parents, some children seem to be comforted by using their brother's or sister's bedroom, thereby experiencing a sense of closeness.

Many children are hesitant and fearful of talking about the dead child because it starts parents crying. This could lead to another member of the family becoming angry, so the child quickly learns not to mention the subject. Equally, children can attempt to protect their parents by not allowing them to go out.

Guilt is an emotion most siblings of whatever age experience. It can arise for a wide range of reasons. Perhaps they see death as a punishment for misbehaviour. One younger brother used to make fun of his slightly retarded older brother until he committed suicide. He now sits by the graveside and asks his brother for advice. Some children might have wished their brother or sister dead. This can be a problem when illness is spread over months and years, creating resentment in a child for the attention the sick child receives. Another guilt reaction occurs when brothers or sisters feel they didn't love the other person enough. Jealousy is normal among brothers and sisters. A common reaction is:

> *'It's not right for me to live when the other person is dead. I should be dead in his place.'*

A four-year-old who lost his brother through cot death said:

> *'If I had been here, my (Fisher Price) medical kit would have saved him.'*

It is common for grandparents to feel that death is some kind of exchange, but this can also be seen in teenagers and young children.

Children can feel guilty because they sense the parents would have preferred them to die rather than their brother or sister. This can lead to numerous behavioural reactions such as temper tantrums, fights with other siblings, lack of interest in school and a general dissatisfaction with their surroundings. Anger and guilt are closely linked. Anger can arise from a wide number of reactions:

- A sense of abandonment that a child has been left by a brother or sister

- A feeling that they are unimportant – why else would their brother or sister leave them?

- A belief that their future has been affected – they have to be the oldest now with no one to follow

- A sense that they have to fight forces much bigger than themselves

Such anger can be directed at a number of people – parents, other children, teachers, or God. It can surface in children of all ages. Cot deaths can raise issues for children. One boy was angry that the babysitter still had her own child even though his brother died at her home. Another small boy would look into other people's prams and say to the parent, 'When will your baby die?'

Miscommunication also raises feelings of anger. In one case, when a boy's brother died through cot death the police were on the scene. The boy asked the policeman if his baby brother would be all right. The policeman said, 'yes'. Later the child showed anger towards policemen because he had not been told the truth.

Children at various ages can create a variety of family problems. When children are young, parents can be far too protective of them. However, parents can also react negatively to a child.

'After the loss of my daughter, when my son was ill I would play it down – saying, "Oh, you'll be okay". I just couldn't face another illness of any kind.'

When the siblings of the bereaved were teenagers, several parents felt they missed out on interest in their schooling.

'My son's cleverness was obscured by the loss. I didn't appreciate his ability.'

When the child who died had been older than the remaining sibling, then a turning point for the parents came when that child reached the age at which death occurred. Obviously, celebration times such as 18th or 21st birthdays or weddings were difficult. A wedding where the best man should have been the groom's brother, now deceased, can be extremely painful.

Also, where a death has occurred as the result of a road accident, the time when younger brothers learn to drive cars or motorbikes can be a frightful time for parents.

'Because of my daughter's car accident, I didn't want my son to drive. I even hoped he'd fail his test.'

However, parents encounter a great release when surviving children reach into new areas of life that the deceased never achieved. One boy dedicated his degree to his decreased brother, a moment of pride for his parents. When children found others who had experienced loss of a brother or sister at the same age, parents said how pleased they were that at least the child had someone to talk to who understood. Parents on the whole explained how difficult it was to leave other children – whether older or younger than the deceased. Many felt they would not have coped without their other children. For those who lost babies and small children, in most cases the families had another baby or babies, thus providing a new focus for the parents. Although the parents still said how deep their pain was in loss, they had the consolation of others to love. If the baby was born with abnormalities, the parents' fear that this would happen again frequently prevented them from having other children. This, however, did not take away their longing for another child.

With older parents who had lost teenagers and grown-up children, the situation was different. By the time couples had recovered even slightly from their loss, for the most part they were too old to begin again with childbirth. In families with other younger children, there was still hope and growth taking place in the family. However, in couples with an only child now dead, or where the youngest had died and brothers or sisters were much older, there seemed a lack of hope and desire for the future. Here, parents seemed far more trapped in the past, compared to the younger families with growing active children. Bereavement seems to have an ageing effect on parents. Hence, the older the bereaved parents the less likely they are to have the energy or desire to build a family afresh.

The role of work

Research has been undertaken to examine whether rumination on the death decreases the sooner a parent gets back to work and into more activity.[24] The results suggest that those who remain at home are more likely to dwell on the loss than others.

Most men felt that work helped because it kept them active and less apathetic. Here was a place where, on the whole, people didn't mention the loss, and if they did it was more in reference to how the wife was doing. A daily regular commitment provided a role for a bereaved parent, compared to being at home, engulfed in memories. This however did not mean emotions were totally suppressed. Several men echoed that they had often felt like crying at work:

'Feelings would suddenly come flooding in and catch you unawares.'

---

[24] A Dyregrov and S Matthiesen, 'Parental Grief following the death of an infant, A follow-up over one year'. *Scandinavian Journal of Psychology*, 1991, Vol 32.

When the topic of loss came up at work, fathers felt people were negative in their approach. Some approaches made them feel guilty – 'Isn't your wife getting better yet,' or 'You need to pull yourself together, put it behind you' – or people asked in a fretful way because they were concerned for their own children.

A few said how supportive people at work had been; perhaps a boss would always send a card on the anniversary, or a former colleague would keep in touch by telephone. It is common for someone at work quietly to share their experience of the loss of their own child. New friendships are often formed because of this identification. For those in leadership positions, there was a unanimous agreement that they had become more sympathetic to other workers' needs:

'At one time I had no sympathy with others having time off work, but now my attitude has changed.'

The sharp contrast between one partner out at work, perhaps with feelings bottled up, and the other partner at home, perhaps spending a large part of the day in tears, comes to a head at tea time. From the interviews, it seemed that the working partner wanted to receive sympathy and support for having to plod on at work, but often found their partner in tears, with little sign of activity having taken place in the home. The pain and anger suppressed at work seemed to be released at home. Unfortunately, the hurt on both sides frequently led to situations that couples could not handle.

Relatives, friends and the neighbourhood

In Baoule villages in West Africa, when a death occurs, relatives and friends gather quickly from the surrounding villages, and as they arrive greet the bereaved with the word, 'NYAKO'.[25] This word is constantly repeated by individuals or groups as they recite words of comfort. In contrast, in the West we seem to have no prescribed words to express our sympathy after a death. Even in the set ritual of the funeral service and wake afterwards, people seem uncomfortable with the bereaved. We seem to have no suitable phrases to convey the feelings of solidarity and compassion in the face of death. Yet it can be the support of others – family and friends – that eases the isolation and anguish of bereavement.

Dr Glenn Vernon asked a thousand college students what they would do if they met someone who had recently lost a loved one. Twenty-five per cent said they would mention the death. Forty per cent said they would prefer that the bereaved brought up the subject. And 25% preferred that the death not be mentioned at all. The remainder had no idea what they would do.[26] This study revealed the feelings in a clearly defined bereavement situation.

---

[25]S Bourg, *When Pregnancy Fails*, Routledge & Keegan, London 1982.

[26]G Vernon, *Sociology of Death: An analysis of Death-Related Behaviour*, Ronald Press, New York, 1970.

But when it comes to the death of a baby or child, friends and relatives are even more uncertain about what to say or do. Clearly, not every family or neighbourhood is the same. Some families are structured as true support systems, while others do not possess these qualities. Instead, they may even create an aberrant atmosphere where the stress associated with loss is exaggerated. Having knowledge of the kind of family that surrounds the individual parent is important in understanding both the impact of child death on the parent and how the parent is likely to respond.

How do parents view the support offered by their relatives, friends and neighbours when a child dies? At first, leading up to the funeral, most families in loss are deluged by telephone calls, cards and flowers. There are many jobs to be done involving doctors, funeral directors and clergy so the parents have contact with professional people. However, after the funeral it is usually left to relatives, friends and the local neighbourhood to continue this care and support.

It became apparent in my interviews that there was no standard response by society to the bereaved but similarities were apparent in the responses parents made about relatives and friends. Perhaps the main message was one of surprise that people do not react as expected. Generally, there seemed to be a difference in how relatives responded compared to neighbours and friends. Although there were a few exceptions where a close knit family proved helpful, overall friends were more supportive than brothers, sisters or parents of the bereaved. This may be a sign of the general change in society where people live in their social enclaves separated by many miles from their close relatives. Therefore, support is found more from those on hand – friends. However, there was a high expectation that relatives, however distant, would get in touch by telephone to offer understanding and support. To the disappointment of many, relatives did not seem to respond adequately to their grief. As one parent explained:

'Family were helpful at first but it's still your tragedy. The intensity of that support goes away very quickly.'

Only 37% of the parents said relatives were helpful, whereas for friends the figure was 75%. Research suggests that 55% of support should come from the environment and community.[27] If this is so, perhaps it is one reason parents struggle on in their grief for such a long time.

'Friends helped me where my husband didn't. Some came and we just talked and talked till four in the morning.'

Sometimes parents were not looking for much support, just understanding.

'Our milkman just looked at me and touched my shoulder, he didn't need to say anything.'

The greatest support was found in tight knit communities where there was a sense of belonging and where people seemed to know everything about each other. Here there was a sense of the community reacting as a family unit. However, most of the people interviewed did not come from such an insulating community. Indeed, some parents found that friends were so unable to

---

[27] J 'Tatlebaum, *The Courage to Grieve*, Lippincott & Crowell, New York, 1980.

cope with what had happened that they ended up in a caring role to others, which only led to greater exhaustion.

One of the main reactions was for people to ignore the fact that a death had occurred. Unfortunately, it becomes impossible to help a grieving friend or relative if you are constantly deviating from the topic. In one family, the relatives chose not to tell the truth to nephews and nieces who assumed their cousin was still alive! Other families found that relatives quickly stopped talking about the dead child, as if to stop reminding the bereaved parents of their loss!

'It's as if people believe if you're not talking about your loss, you're not thinking about it, yet it is the one thing you are constantly thinking about.'

When relatives forget about anniversaries and birthdays, parents feel especially aggrieved and let down. If there are problems in the wider family beforehand, death seems only to highlight the situation and distance the relatives rather than create a healing situation. Degrees of negative reaction vary among relatives, from those who keep a stiff upper lip and never again mention the child's name to those who feel the parents are wallowing in self-pity and need to pull themselves together. However, sometimes surprises are discovered. Perhaps a grandparent would reveal that they had lost a child many years ago. News of this death had never been shared before in the family. When this occurs, it tends to provide an opportunity for a deepening bond to form between parents and grandparents.

The role of close friends, which parents might well have thought would be an asset, proves to many to be a great disappointment. It is not only distant acquaintances who seem remote but many long-standing friends.

'I wanted to talk to my family and friends but I realised they didn't want to.'

'It's as if you are contagious, people don't want their child to catch it.'

'My child died of a reaction to aspirin. One mother made an enormous fuss at school in case it was contagious. It made me feel very annoyed.'

It seems that parents with children the same age as the deceased find it especially hard to cope. Rather than face the reality that they can lose a baby or child, they seem to pretend it can't happen to them. Continuing to see their friends in loss only reveals their vulnerability; therefore they withdraw to a safe distance.

Certainly, those who are in loss are not the best of company. There is a tendency for the parent to talk about the loved one, the illness, the doctor, the memories, and soon friends seem not to have the patience to continue to care. One mother felt especially vulnerable at Christmas:

'Everyone is busy preparing to celebrate and relax; they don't want your tragedy spoiling their Christmas.'

Having interviewed many parents I almost felt they had all been primed to relate one recurring experience: that people would cross the street to avoid speaking to them. As one honest neighbour put it:

'When I saw you coming towards me I wished I could have dug a hole and disappeared.'

This highlights the chronic inability of our society to face up to such tragedies and to express our feelings. It is clearly not that people don't care, more their inability to show positive support adequately and sensibly. People seem therefore to fall into three categories in regard to their reaction: withdrawal from the survivors; comparing, evaluating and judging; and eliciting sympathy.

Withdrawal from the survivors

After a funeral, the parents need continual support. Unfortunately, it seems that this is the time when people withdraw, especially where the illness has been prolonged. Others seem to think that once the funeral is over parents should bury their feelings and get on with life. But the bereaved need people who can offer consistent comfort and consolation, who are willing to talk over what has occurred, or who can reminisce about some important moments in the loved child's life.

Comparing, evaluating and judging

People say remarkable things to those who are in immense shock:

- ❤ 'Pull yourself together.'
- ❤ 'Your grandchild will be like him, it will help.'
- ❤ 'You'll soon get over it.'
- ❤ 'Are you still crying?'
- ❤ 'How are things, you must be better now?'
- ❤ 'You've got another son, why be so upset.'
- ❤ 'You've got to let go.'
- ❤ Well, at least you didn't get to know him.'
- ❤ 'Time will heal.'
- ❤ 'It would have been better if he hadn't been born,'
  (This person's child had been 16 years of age.)

When babies die, people seem to assume that having another child will cancel the loss. The problem is, the grieved do not want to feel better or to replace the child with anyone else. What people fail to realise is that, with miscarriages or the loss of babies, a major tragedy has occurred – probably the worst so far in a person's life. The parents themselves are not really sure how to act. How do you grieve for someone who existed in mental images and perhaps in internal movements? Their feelings are filled with contradictions and ambiguities. For instance, if it was the first pregnancy, they wonder, 'are they parents or aren't they?' Also, other people are unable to converse about the situation for they have no memory of the baby to relate to.

Parents who are mourning the loss of a premature baby receive a strong message from society that their loss is not significant. Sad, yes, but not really tragic. 'At least you can have another one.' The comments of others make a bereaved parent begin to question his or her own feelings and then try to tailor them to the perceived expectations of others.

'You quickly learn to be an actress, to put on a face.'

'I found myself caught in my reactions, for if I appeared to be happy people thought I had got over it like a cold.'

Equally devastating are suggestions that the death could have been prevented; the hospital or treatment was wrong, or even perhaps that the child wasn't wanted. Parents of cot death victims or suicides are vulnerable here. No judgements will bring back the loved one or help the survivor. Indeed, the parents experience enough guilt as it is without the neighbourhood adding to it. A mother who lost a child through choking on a sweet found that the mums at the school became extremely difficult to relate to. She sensed that all around her, parents were judging with their eyes!

Eliciting sympathy

In an effort to show their sorrow and empathy, some people display their own grief and talk about how they too have been affected by loss. They think that they understand because of their own experience.

'I know how you feel.'

'My cat died, I know.'

'Oh, divorce is much worse.'

Others begin to share their experiences of loss, particularly in miscarriages. However, such comments only rankle with the bereaved 'like a knife turning in them'. In most cases, people's comments hurt without them realising. This sometimes happens when people don't know that loss has taken place. A mum, after losing her daughter, was out shopping with her only son, when a person said, 'Is he your only one? Have another to keep him company.'

Often, in general conversation, people ask, 'How many children do you have?' This creates a dilemma for parents. Do they mention the deceased child, which then embarrasses the questioner, or do they ignore the deceased, only to feel guilty and ashamed later for letting their child down.

When I was a hospital maternity Chaplain, I found that women demonstrate their experience of miscarriage by including the dead baby in the number of their family, but would acknowledge that they did not raise the issue outside. As a mother said, 'I don't know how to tell people in a subtle way, so they can cope. Now I say, I've got two children, but I had three.'

Those bereaved of children do find that some people previously on the fringe of their lives replace the close friends who withdraw after death. Although they may end up with a much smaller number of close friends, they are at least more likely to be available and supportive.

The funeral of Amy, a stillborn baby, held in the hospital chapel.

8

The Funeral

Blessed are they that mourn,
For they shall be comforted.

Matthew 5:4

When someone we love dies, particularly a child who has been dependent on us, one of our strongest emotions is likely to be sheer panic. We feel helpless. We don't know what to do. Dimly, we are aware that arrangements will have to be made but we don't know what they are or how to go about them. Flowers and cards begin arriving and there are endless telephone calls to be made, informing people of what happened and when the funeral is to take place. The days leading up to the funeral are full of furious activity:

- Finding a funeral director
- Visiting the child at the Chapel of Rest
- Obtaining the death certificate
- Informing relatives and friends
- Registering the death
- Opening up your home to visitors
- Opening the mail and condolence cards
- Arranging the funeral
- Informing the newspaper
- Ordering flowers
- Caring for the family

Before embarking on the process of planning and arranging details, it is far better simply to be a parent in loss. All of this long list can wait, certainly hours if not a day or two. Those who are able to be with their deceased child, to sit with, hold, kiss and talk to it, find benefits in the long run. Those moments of sitting with the child can never be regained.

Parents seem to find a remarkable inner strength which sees them through the first few days. When they are about to meet doctors, funeral directors, clergy, clerk to the registry, let alone the police, they need to tap inner resources. That is why it is helpful to have a supportive relative or friend, slightly removed from the situation. They can take in detail which a parent is not able to concentrate on. This is important, especially with accidents. To have a friend calmly finding out the facts can help later when a parent is trying to deal with the consequences, especially if it involves legal action.

Planning the funeral

When it comes to planning a funeral service for a child of whatever age, it is helpful to take your time with the decisions. A funeral director and religious leader will normally visit you. They will outline some of the decisions that need to be taken:

- Would you like people to be able to visit the child in the Chapel of Rest?
- Do you prefer burial or cremation?
- Will there be a service in Church?
- Do you want the hearse to go via a special place, such as the school?
- Who will carry the coffin?
- Will the coffin be in Church before you arrive, or will the family follow it into the building?
- What music would be appropriate?
- What hymns would you like?
- Would you like the child's favourite piece of music played, e.g., a pop song?
- Shall a friend, relative or school teacher say a few words about the child?
- Shall the service be recorded?
- Would you like the child to be buried with a grandparent?
- Would you like to throw the soil into the grave?
- Would you like the other children to share their views about the service?
- Would you like the other children to place one flower each on the coffin or into the grave?
- Would you like flowers to be all of one type?
- Would you like a record of all who attend the service?
- Would you like donations to go to a charity?

Parents can leave many of these decisions to the professionals, or shape the plans themselves. It is understandable that the funeral directors and ministers of religion like quick decisions as they are busy people. However, it is important that parents take time to reflect, perhaps asking professionals to return another day for the answers. There is always something personal and special about an individual child which, if conveyed, can enhance a funeral. But the minister may miss this unless a parent has time to reflect and communicate it to him.

With relatives in a state of shock and yet with many practical arrangements to be completed, there can be tension in a family about making the arrangements. When a baby or young child dies, it is unlikely that the family has had any experience at arranging funerals and there also seems to be a sacredness which distances people from helping.

Content of service

The content of the service at a funeral is different for a baby and – say – an older teenager. There is far less to refer to in a baby's life and therefore the funeral focuses more always on the grief of the parents. When older children die, their friends can help by recommending a song, favourite poem or reading that the parents knew nothing about. For teenagers, there are plenty of experiences to refer to and people are generally willing to say a few words about the child. A school teacher or a youth group leader may be asked speak on behalf of the organisation and will relate to the mourners associated with that group. I have sometimes moved outside at the end of the service and released a helium balloon as a symbol of letting the child's spirit rise to new life. It can be most beneficial if parents let go of the string themselves.

One noticeable difference between a small child's funeral and that of a teenager or adult is the size of the coffin. A baby's coffin is a small white box. The petite size can be a psychological shock to the mourners. The smallness of the coffin seems to bring home to them the overwhelming impact of the injustice of a life cut short.

It is common for parents to carry the coffin of a baby or younger child into church and for friends to carry older teenagers. This is an interesting reversal of the trend for funeral directors to carry the coffin. Somehow, when it comes to the death of young people, tradition seems to have its head and assist those involved in the grief process.

I once performed a thanksgiving service for a severely mentally handicapped boy in his late teens. Since the home mates of the boy had been unable to attend the funeral, the second service provided an opportunity for them to identify with their friend. However, communication was limited due to the extreme mental handicap of the mourners. Visual aids were needed to simplify the service and to enable the friends to link in with their memories of their close friend.

If a will has been produced then the executors need to be involved, for the will can specify what arrangements the deceased requested. Often, with the elderly, a partner or son has discussed what their loved one would like at his or her funeral. When it comes to the death of a younger person, confusion prevails and it is unlikely that a will exists.

Cremation or burial?

There is no right or wrong choice with regard to cremation or burial. When a child dies, this is an issue that will probably never have been discussed. Out of those interviewed, only one mother had ever spoken to her son and therefore knew of his preference. Usually, parents have formulated their views on such matters at a much earlier time in their lives. What is helpful is to have a place to visit that represents your memories of the child. This may be a burial site, a place where the ashes were scattered or perhaps where a parent has planted a tree in remembrance.

The general trend is to prefer cremation. In cremation, the body is clearly disposed of and the process completed with the burial or scattering of the ashes. But with the burial of a coffin there is a feeling in some parents' minds that the process is not complete.

'I felt hurt in winter that he was out there in the cold.'

One mother had not visited the grave for sixteen years; when she did visit she said:

'I felt as if he had just died, and burst into tears.'

Those who choose burial seem to find both benefits and problems. The custom in the UK is that after the burial of the body, the guests view the flowers sent and then depart to the next of kin for food and drink. Some parents wanted to stay longer at the grave side when others had left, but felt constrained by expectations to leave. A few families seemed to fear that the mother would always be visiting the graveside and this might delay her recovery. However, the majority of mothers not only visited regularly but found it a source of comfort and strength.

The graveside visits seem on the whole to give comfort to the bereaved and allow others like grandparents and other children, a chance to visit and reflect at a later time. However, the decision about what to place on to the headstone can be a headache for some, with parents leaving it more than a year to decide because of hesitation or disagreement between partners.

Flowers

When a funeral takes place for an elderly person, it is common to find that the deceased, or the family, wish to have a limited number of flowers present. With the death of the young, however, many relatives seem to believe the more flowers the better. In one service, the family requested only daffodils as this had been the favourite flower of the dead child. The parents found it a comfort to find the church awash in yellow.

When older children die, the floral arrangements can represent a particular interest or hobby the child had. Two funerals that I personally ministered come to mind. Both were for older teenagers killed suddenly. One boy had played football for a local factory team. The other had been heavily involved in scooters. Both funerals were full to over the capacity of the Church (seven hundred people), with many standing in the aisles. Scores of flower arrangements arrived, created in the appropriate themes of footballs or scooters. In both cases, the care people had taken in producing such floral sprays gave great comfort to the parents.

Keeping a record

Parents take great comfort in the number of people who attend the funeral service and want to keep a record of attendance. Cards can be provided for the congregation to fill in. However, many people come without pens and so leave the cards blank. A better alternative is to buy a special book that people sign as they come into Church. Either the funeral director or the Church has to manage this, as people often arrive extra early for children's funerals.

On some occasions I have recorded a funeral service. Parents struggle to take in what is said at a service, so it can be useful at a later date. In a few cases, a relative who lives a long distance away has been unable to attend and has requested a tape. Those who have a recording seem to be pleased to have it. However, none had felt inclined or able to listen to it afterwards. Even if parents never listen to the tape, it can be a comfort as it represents a link with the past. One parent specifically wished the service had been taped for she felt her memory dishonoured the event: she particularly wanted to recall what the Minister had said to the mourners.

Funeral directors

Parents I spoke with had mixed feelings about funeral directors. Some felt that it was just a business to the funeral director, who therefore only went through the motions. Others found their funeral director to be most helpful and caring. What needs to be acknowledged is that – as with any of the professionals who deal with the death of a baby or child, whether medical, clerical or a funeral director – there is a reluctance to get too close because of the awkwardness of the situation. Funeral directors themselves acknowledge that they find dealing with babies and children most upsetting. This sense of pain can in some cases cause the professional to withdraw sooner from the client than they perhaps otherwise would have done.

At times funeral directors may find themselves at the receiving end of a bereaved person's anger. One lady found that at first she couldn't cope with all the practical questions put to her by the funeral director. She finally erupted, 'I just don't care.'

When young children die, where the family was just beginning to make its way financially, the sudden cost of a funeral can create worry and tension. Most of the people I interviewed sincerely wanted the very best for the funeral of the child, yet many were concerned at the cost.

The family gathering

The family get together after the funeral proves to be a release for people and their emotions. As one father put it:

'Afterwards we laughed together which released the pressure we all felt.'

It can however be strange for bereaved parents to be entertaining on the day of the child's funeral. One mother felt how ridiculous it was that she was going around trying to cheer everyone up. 'I laughed at something,' she said, 'and people looked at me as if shocked.'

Although such gatherings tend to be family affairs, one point seems to jar in the parents' memories – when a relative is not present. When others, for example nurses, make an effort to attend the funeral and the gathering afterwards, it only highlights the hurt when a relative doesn't attend.

'Our Scottish relatives didn't attend the funeral, so have never really understood our grief. The relationship has never been the same since.'

All parents expressed their deep thanks to those who stood alongside them, whether by attending the funeral or by supporting them at a later date. As one father put it:

'Somehow the funeral was right, we were at the right place with the right people.'

The funeral provides a sense of climax and release, after the family has prepared for it for days. Somehow, the parents seem to get by, and with the help of various professionals such as doctors, funeral directors and clergy, reach the stage where the funeral is behind them.

'Somehow we calmly talked ourselves through it.'

9

The Role of Religion

The wind bloweth where it listeth,

and thou hearest the sound thereof

but canst not tell whence it cometh, and whither it goeth;

so is everyone that is born of the Spirit.

John 3:8

A child's death seems a strange, unnatural disaster. It perplexes us and makes us aware that, in the end, we have no power to control our own lives or our children's. Inevitably, parents attempt to search for some reason for the loss and many questions are raised in their minds as they dwell on the child's death, trying to find some comfort, peace and hope.

- Is the death fate, or just bad luck?

- Where is my loved child now?

- Does he still exist in some form that I can relate to?

- What happens to the personality of the child?

- If there is life beyond death will I recognise my child, or will she continue to grow and change?

There have been many different beliefs about what actually happens after death takes place.[28] Whatever their previous religious beliefs, parents come into bereavement with some already loosely formed views. However, when we lose someone as precious as a child – of whatever age – all of these preconceived views are challenged. A study in America showed that a majority of parents (about 70%) actually turn to their religious faith for answers and for comfort.[29] In the questionnaire completed in Britain, the findings seemed to reveal different results.

---

[28]R Grainger, *The Unburied*, Churchman, London, 1988.

[29]R Knapp, *Beyond Endurance, op cit.*

Eighty-four per cent said that their belief in God had remained the same or increased and only 16% said their faith had decreased.

When looking at people's religious reactions after the loss of a loved one it is important to recognise the differences in national culture even in one religious denomination. Often, when figures are quoted for the effects of faith on a parent in bereavement, they are taken from one culture. It is easy to misinterpret results and assume they relate to the same denomination in other cultures. There is a danger that we read what is the norm for bereavement reaction in, for example, America and assume it will be the same in Britain. Religion is just one example where caution ought to be taken and more respect given to the cultural influences in differing areas.

The survey in America suggests that parents are so overpowered by a tragedy which is incomprehensible, that they turn in desperation to a religious interpretation to find justification for the situation. It found that about 30% of the parents interviewed responded to some form of genuine religious revitalisation or conversion experience.[30] In other cases, it took the form of a rekindling of the belief in some sort of reunion with the child after the parent's own death. However, following one-to-one interviews with parents in Britain, it seems clear that most parents keep the faith they started with, although it may vary slightly in intensity. What is clear is that parents do venture on a search for some reason behind the event.

> *'It was all for something, although I don't know what. I get annoyed if someone says, "It was all for nothing".'*

In some cases, parents do seem to deepen their belief in God. In such situations, in the early days of bereavement God seems close to them, which assists them in this difficult period.

> *'People say how can you believe in God now? But I say how can you not believe?'*

However, others felt especially let down by God, despite continuing in their weakened faith.

> *'When I need God, I feel it's as if He puts up his shutters.'*

Although parents were angry with God, this did not surface as much as expected. Believers were frustrated at the thought that God seemed to be saying the child was OK, when parents felt such enormous loss.

> *'How can my child be all right? If he was, he would be next to me — not with God.'*

Many said that they still had faith in a God but somehow the belief had been changed.

> *'Our faith has been pulled to shreds. It is now back together, but certainly not as it was before.'*

> *'Our attitude has changed. God didn't make it happen, yet He didn't prevent it. I now see a picture of life with free will and a God without power.'*

Some of those who had no real belief in a God, whether before or afterwards, revealed how

---

[30]*ibid..*

envious they were of those who had faith and how they would value this belief if they could but find it.

One recurring theme was of parents who would acknowledge that they struggled to believe in God after the death of their child, but nevertheless strongly believed in an afterlife. Eighty-one per cent said they believed in an afterlife, compared to 74% who believed in a God. Of those who had Church contact, many stressed the difficulty of worshipping in a Church. The hymns and prayers conjured up so many thoughts and memories that parents found it too painful. Others continued to pray to God for their child even if they had lost their understanding of and belief in an intervening God.

After six months to one year, several parents searched for their child by going to see a spiritualist or medium. Some found this a comfort, although none of the parents interviewed continued with the contact. In some cases, it seemed the medium was able to be accurate about the deceased's life, which brought comfort to the parent. In other cases, whatever the parents were looking for, they did not find it, and so were still left with big questions.

When the death of a child occurs, it raises many imponderables. The natural assumption, at least in a Western society, is that children will out-live their parents. So when a child dies it has an effect like no other death. The death of parents and grandparents, although tragic, is somehow expected in the flow of life. Older people have lived out their story, and although no one wants the story to draw a close, it is accepted that every story has an ending. However, when a child dies it shatters all our presuppositions about life. Such a death makes us ask why someone so young should die rather than ourselves. The plans, hopes and aspirations that we invest in our children's future evaporate and take with them our own drive and energy for the future.

Society has placed its trust in a god of medicine and science only to see it fail. Even the old God of Christianity can seem strangely silent. In the past, the role of religion was very much one of caring for people in their own homes. This involved both prayer and physical, emotional and mental support. There was a clear purpose of providing hope to a patient, whether it was through overcoming the illness or facing death courageously and victoriously with the certainty of Heaven to come.

Elaine Tierney notes that in the thirteenth century popular preaching instructed parishioners to remember death:

> Gollfried wrote: 'Preachers advised people to go to sleep every night as if it was their last and as if their beds were their tombs.' Thomas à Kempis wrote of death: 'He who is dead to the world, is not in the world, but in God, unto whom he lives, comfortable, and your life is hid with Christ in God.' Preparation for death was important. To die without having confessed one's sins would submit one to eternal damnation. So the emphasis was on death, and from this developed the concept of dying well, what the guides described as the 'art of dying.' [31]

---

[31]Quoted in S. Hauerwas, *Naming the Silences*, Eerdmans, Michigan, 1990.

Yet today many people want to die quickly and painlessly, without causing trouble to those close to them. We echo this attitude by seeing hospitals and hospices as the place to die, away from home, in the hands of the medical world. Cancer seems to be our greatest fear as it represents a painful death to endure.

In the past, the Christian teaching spoke far more about the importance of suffering, of taking up your cross, and learning through difficult times. Today, science too allows suffering. However, here it is tied to the hope that a little suffering through chemotherapy or radiation treatment will lead to a healing in this world. Hope is forever present in both Christian and scientific ideologies. There is the Christian hope that even when the inevitable strikes and death occurs there is always eternal life, a new Kingdom and a new beginning. Today, the new god of science also has hope. At first, it does much to pretend that death is not occurring. However, an American survey reveals graphically how even terminally ill children can see through this false veneer. [32]. Then there is the hope that one day we will find an answer which will prevent further deaths from a particular disease. Even the bereaved parents become involved in this hope as many carry out charity work to raise finance to support this research. Our physicians have become warriors engaged in combat with the ultimate adversary – death! Those who die young are held up as sacrificial lambs, who die for the good of those to come! Of course, since this is a war that cannot be won, it puts doctors in a peculiar double bind. They must do everything they can to keep us alive, as if living were an end in itself, but then they must endure our blame when, inevitably, they fail.

Here we come full circle, where bereaved parents find themselves now blaming the new god of science instead of the old Christian God. Yet however much parents blame the medical profession for failure, they find themselves equally unable to let go of their faith. They find themselves supporting the hospitals with time and money. In the same way, those who had a Christian faith beforehand find themselves, although sometimes greatly weakened in their faith initially, still praying, even if they are not sure to whom they are praying!

The problem with medicine is not only that it is unable to remove the inevitable – the fact of death – but that it may be unaware of what is actually the best for a patient. What is required is full perspective of a person's needs, which takes into account not only their physical illness but also the whole context of the person and their family. Only then can we perceive what may be right for a patient, especially a child. Any diagnosis must include the reality that death is a part of life, and therefore may be the most appropriate course for the patient. Perhaps it is here that the god of medicine seems to fail to achieve a holistic approach by not fully accepting the inevitability of death.

---

[32] M Bluebond-Langer, *The Private Worlds of Dying Children*, Princeton, New Jersey, 1978.

Parents with seriously ill children find themselves facing a cocktail of differing ideologies. There are the various views of doctors and nurses, some of whom seek to continue treatment regardless of the outcome, while others wish to acknowledge the limits of their treatment and withdraw to a discrete distance, allowing the family to perform their skills of love and care in their own home.

When death does occur, parents have to face various street theologies which suggest that the child is in heaven and will remain a child until reunited with its parents, or perhaps the child is looking down upon the parents and caring for them, or even being looked after in Heaven by deceased grandparents. Alternatively, there are those who want to be caring but must make sure the parents understand that, in their eyes, the child is no more and therefore needs to be forgotten as a soon as possible.

But what about the main religion of our country? We might expect the role of Christianity to have quite a lot to say, especially since it is based on a Godly father who Himself lost a Son! So often at funerals and later on, those of the Christian faith seek to convey their enthusiasm for the concept of the Resurrection at a time when the bereaved parents want their child with them now and not in Heaven. Regardless of Heaven's reality and the hope in the future for reunion, parents want to talk with their child now; they want to see it, hug it, and listen to its plans for the future. The fact that a child is in good hands does not put it back into its mother's and father's hands where it ought to be.

Despite this, the Christian faith does have much to say on the subject of loss. It is not the purpose of this book to go deeply into theology, as that would be a book in itself. Books that readers may find thought-provoking and beneficial are listed in Appendix III. However, it seems to me that the Christian message has a great deal to offer bereaved parents. This is a message that is indeed connected with the concept of a Heaven and a future life. But this part of the Christian heritage needs to be reserved for parents who are in a frame of mind to begin to absorb such concepts and who have already travelled some distance down the road of grief. The main message of the Christian faith is one of a God that is not distant but draws near, not only through His Son's suffering on the cross and dying; but through His followers who are also willing to suffer in their pastoral care of those in need. In talking to many bereaved parents, it does seem to most that a God that suffers for them is appreciated but, by itself, somehow not comforting enough. To mention the resurrection can for some be taken as an insult, for they want their child now, not just in the future. Where Christianity has made the biggest impact is where Christians have practised what they preach by not only drawing alongside the bereaved, but sticking with them for years through their grief. This is both costly in time and in our own faith, for it leaves us in situations where we do not have cheap answers to give but rather a willingness to sit alongside and mourn with our friend. Let me finish this chapter with a story which illustrates my point.

The place is the neo-natal unit of a hospital. As I enter the ward, there is the sound of machinery labouring to keep alive almost lifeless forms. The noise is frightening to the uninitiated, and so is the sight. Complicated equipment surrounds tiny babies and creates an intimidating picture. Tubes, IV bottles, wires, drainage jars, oscilloscopes, heart stimulators, blood pressure monitors, and respirators are everywhere. When we home in on one premature baby weighing three pounds, we see plasma and glucose drips into both tiny arms. Oxygen is fed into both nostrils. A respirator tube down his throat stretches his mouth, creating an unnatural appearance. A blood pressure cuff on his wrist is continuously feeding results to a digital monitor next to the incubator. Electrocardiogram patches dot his little chest and there is a little gauze pad covering his eyes. The room is full of buzzing, hissing, wheezing, thumping noises of the support machinery. If you stand close to the baby, you can hear the air being pushed into and extracted from its lungs by the respirator. When I am called to the ward, it is obvious which incubator to go to as it is surrounded by a doctor, two nurses and the baby's parents. As a flood of light flashes from the monitoring equipment and beeps erupt, it is clear that this baby is close to death.

My role in all of this confusion is to take the parents into a small private room while the nurse removes all of the hi-tech equipment from the baby. I quietly listen to the parents' story, while out of sight the nurse puts some baby clothes on the infant and lifts him gently into a wicker basket. Just before the baby is brought in to the parents, a doctor briefly explains that there is nothing medicine can now do for their child. As the baby is brought in, the doctor and the nurse leave. In the silence behind the closed door I sit with mum and dad and their dying baby. My role as chaplain is to encourage the parents to pick their baby up, perhaps for the first time. How strange that the first opportunity to hold your child is in death. Silently, we observe the beauty of this tiny creature. A nurse pops in and takes a photograph, almost as if it were a birthday! The minutes tick by as we wait. Despite being without the machinery, the baby continues to breath shallowly for several more minutes. We don't know the precise second when the baby passes into eternity. We continue to sit, almost taking turns to cry, to embrace one another and to hold onto the baby. Minutes pass by, yet it seems eternity. I say a short prayer, and finally a nurse suggests that it is time for the parents to let go of their baby, at least physically, and return home. Reluctantly they obey, as ever. The hospital ward is cleaned up and prepared for the next arrival. The parents go home in a daze into a community unprepared for their news. As I venture home myself, I wonder what I have achieved or communicated. It seems that I have said nothing and achieved nothing. Yet, somehow, it seems to have been a privilege to have been there . . . almost rewarding.

Section 3

The Way Ahead

When the death of a child strikes a family, it creates a state of panic and chaos. Even when there is some anticipation of the loss, nevertheless the lives of the family will never be the same. It is rather like throwing a pack of cards up into the air and letting them fall. The cards are totally disorientated. This is how parents feel about their loss.

Most have no experience of other people in this condition, therefore they are ill prepared for what lies ahead. The nearest a person comes to such a devastating loss is when a spouse dies. However, even here the situation is different as a partner has usually achieved a great deal before death.

Our natural reaction when disorientated is quickly to pull ourselves together and get on with life. But here lies the real difficulty for the bereaved. Instead of becoming re-oriented over 100 metres, they find themselves in a marathon. Not only do parents find that they do not want to move forward in life, but they lack the energy and ability to do so. It is sad to meet so many parents asking the question, 'When will I feel better?' as if one day they will wake up cured of the pain and grief. There does not seem to be a sufficient number of experienced counsellors around to help them see that it is a long, slow process. This is why support groups such as The Compassionate Friends and the National Child Death Helpline can be of such help. Here, the parents can share experiences and receive advice on how to cope. There is a greater willingness to accept such comments from fellow companions in grief than from a counsellor, who has in reality never sat where they are sitting, and so can never fully understand.

Support in the early months of bereavement is essential, especially when the parents are feeling so unmotivated. Support is required to enable the bereaved to believe there is a light at the end of the tunnel and that it is worthwhile pushing towards it. However, parents need to realise that recovery is not automatic but requires perseverance and hard work. To be able to come through the tunnel in one piece, a parent needs to accept and face the fact that there will be many turns in the tunnel when they will see no light at the end. To reach the light, they will have to encounter deeper pain than they first realised. But with love and support parents can reach the point of living again. Living always with the pain of their loss, yes, but also being able to move forward with joy and purpose.

Marcus, aged 18, who died of a heart attack after scoring a hat-trick

10

How Can Parents and Siblings Cope?

It is eight weeks, beloved, since you died.
You left the stiffening inert lump of clay
That was no longer you,
And cried aloud in ecstasy
And suddenly I knew
That all that we believed in,
Lived for, told the world,
Had at its smallest count
Some measure that was true.

It is eight months, beloved, since you died,
And out of my aloneness I have woven strength
To build anew;
For all there was of truth in our relationship
Had eddied, grown, intensified,
Till with a clarion call it sounds at the far
reaches of the world
There is no death, no separation of the ways
If man to love prove true.

It is eight years, beloved, since you died.
And for eternity a part of you
is in its essence me.
I know you are, and in that certainty
is woven all the fabric of life.
Gone is all sense of urgency and haste;
For all time now, our spirits meet in time.
Loving, we are no longer bound by love;
Heart of my heart, we've set each other free.

Anonymous

These are some guidelines which parents and other children can follow which I hope will assist them as they journey into bereavement.

The first week

The first few days of bereavement for parents of a child who dies at any age are totally bewildering. It is as if life itself has stopped. There are moments of numbness and shock, outbursts of tears and disbelief. It is extremely important for parents to realise that they cannot cope alone with this burden. As personal as the tragedy may be, they need all the support they can get. Hence, it is advantageous to have loved ones around, who can assure the parents that they are cared for and, regardless of the death, still valued.

Parents needs to know that it is okay to react in whatever way they feel like at the time. It may be they want to run around caring for visitors and making tea, to cry with friends, to laugh at their memories, to be angry at so many things, or to be alone in the child's bedroom. A child's room can be a safe place and the nearest a parent can feel to the child, surrounded by its clothes, possessions and smells. It is helpful to talk about the events of the death, perhaps over and over again. It is exhausting to talk constantly about the loss, but it is helpful as it brings home the reality of the event.

Jean Richardson, in her book, *A Death In the Family*, talks of how some people announce in the local paper that they want 'no letters'.[33] However, all those interviewed said how positive the they found the experience of receiving letters. It was common to receive 'enormous posts'. Since the death of a young person is generally highlighted in the local press, bereaved parents who have experienced their own loss frequently write with words of identification and sympathy. This proved to be comforting indeed for parents, discovering that others around them could understand how they felt. Most parents I met had in fact kept the cards and letters regardless of how long ago their child had died.

'I kept all of the cards and letters. They were most important to me and became precious as they were all I had left afterwards.'

With such an enormous loss as well as so much to plan, it is common for doctors to offer tranquillisers to parents to help them with their nerves and enable them to get to sleep. This seems fine, provided it does not continue for months and months, without any attempt to reduce the parents' dependency. What is important is that parents make sure they take in food, even if it is in small amounts. It may be better to get some fresh air and sleep for short periods rather than rely on pills. A change in sleeping and eating habits is understandable, but parents have to work at keeping both regular.

---

[33]Jean Richardson, *A Death in the Family*, Lion Publishing, Oxford, 1979.

In the midst of their own grief, it is so easy for parents to fail to perceive the needs of other children in the family. They too are going through the same process as their parents. Indeed, a sibling's death raises even more questions for the children.

❤ How should I behave?

❤ Should I cry in public?

❤ When ought I go back to school?

❤ Will I die in the same way?

❤ What is wrong with my parents?

❤ Should I go to the funeral?

❤ Is this happening to me?

❤ Is it my fault?

What is so important is that parents have an open relationship with their children. Obviously, this is difficult to achieve if relationships are tense through lack of communication even before illness and death enter the home. Difficult relationships in families before death so often seem to become even more problematic afterwards. This is why it is helpful for children to have another adult – a grandparent, aunt or friend – to support them in their bewilderment when the parents themselves are in a state of shock.

Eventually parents must begin to relate to and support their remaining children with signs of assurance and care. Children's questions cannot be avoided, even if parents feel unsure of the answers. It is far better to say, 'I don't know why,' than to make up a false story. If parents are able to let the children know that they too have fears, but that together they will survive, then it is more likely to lead to a closer family unit. Children of all ages will need advice, especially during the first few days as they encounter death and bereavement for the first time. It is helpful if parents can always make sure children have a safe place to retreat to when the house is besieged by visitors, and that there is an adult free and able to take care of them.

Practical questions regarding the funeral will need to be answered. I find that parents try to protect children from a funeral when in fact children are more than able to face such situations. (I encourage parents to allow children to the funerals of grandparents so that they gain experience before they, as adults, have to face their parents' death.) Surviving children can feel they have let their brother or sister down by not attending. Years later, they can still be bearing guilt for not being there. Obviously, if children specifically state that they do not want to go then their wish must be respected, provided parents realise that children pick up their 'vibes' very quickly. Is it your child's decision or is it what they think you want? If a child is to attend the service, then a parent can ease the situation by taking the child into the Church a day earlier to acquaint them with the surroundings and explain exactly what will happen, thus removing the fears and barriers.

Children can actually be of help in arranging a funeral, for they can remember favourite things about their brother or sister which can be incorporated into the service. As an example, parents sometimes want to have their deceased child dressed in a favourite costume. Brothers and sisters can well decide what to put in the coffin alongside the child, for example, toys or a favourite possession.

If children are to visit the Chapel of Rest, they do need to be told what to expect. The experience is far less frightening than parents expect, and in fact it can assist other children to come to terms with the reality that their brother or sister is dead.

It helps to let a child know that it is all right to cry at a funeral and yet to laugh at the family gathering afterwards. This can be very confusing for a child unless explained. I cannot emphasise strongly enough the need for a safe room where a child may go during the gathering after the funeral. They too need moments to be alone. Sometimes, families find it helpful for young children to attend the Church service and then to go home and visit the crematorium or burial place later when all is quiet, just with parents. Whatever is decided, children's own views need to be considered. We can so easily put our own fears into them if we are not careful.

Parents can help their surviving children by informing the school of the situation. A sensitive teacher will provide space, both emotionally and practically, for a bereaved child. Some schools even set aside a room where the child can go accompanied by a special teacher.

The months ahead

The days after the funeral often find a parent left alone. Relatives and friends have returned to work and children have gone back to school. From a situation with lots of visitors the house is now strangely silent. A parent is now about to embark on a long trail of coming to terms with reality. One of the hardest tasks for a parent is to accept that the loss is real, that their child will not be returning home. It is in the loneliness of one's own home, with the dead child's possessions all around, that the depth of pain becomes apparent. The process of coming to terms with such a loss can be so lengthy that parents can only cope by taking each day as it comes.

The more parents acknowledge that they need support over this long period, the easier the passage of time will be. Parents need more than just the close family to help them survive. There is a role for a friend who is willing to listen, while others can assist more practically with tasks and errands such as shopping, ironing, and driving the children to activities. Parents seem to feel that they will one day suddenly feel better. However, hard work is required if they are to reach a healthy state again.

This is a dilemma for parents because on one hand they feel like doing nothing except burying their heads under the bedclothes, while at the same time they actually need to work at eating, sleeping in small doses, getting fresh air, etc. This is why they need friends to encourage them. At first, the activity may be small each day, but the more they persevere, the more parents can find themselves performing some duties they would not have expected to do a few months previously. Many parents said they found it beneficial just to get out of the house and walk. The physical activity helps the body, while the mind is free to meander where it will.

It helps to realise that there are things to work at on a regular basis. Having a set time to visit the grave gives a feeling of purpose. Buying something in the name of the remembered child each week can help – for example, flowers for the graveside, a plant for the house, a piece of music the child would have liked. Making a set time to talk to a partner and children can help and can prevent tension from developing when one partner wants to talk while the other wants to avoid the issue. When one partner is at work and another at home, the meeting point at the end of the day can be fraught. Having a set time each day in which a couple both agree to talk can help. This is also true for children as they will need their questions answered over and over again. The more a family can talk about what they find the hardest at a particular time, the greater the help they can be to each other. It helps for couples to take turns at explaining how they feel. This helps to clarify their roles on alternate days – one caring, the other grieving, and vice versa.

A great degree of understanding is required from parents, both in the family and out in the community. At home family members must come to terms with the fact that grief divides and isolates. People grieve in their own way. Where one is depressed and inactive, another may be over active. One wants to talk, while another remains silent. One spends time in the child's bedroom, while another will not venture there. One wants the comfort of touch and sex, while another pushes the partner away.

Space to react in your own way requires extra understanding and acceptance of each other. In addition, bereaved parents need to understand the reactions of their friends and the community. Unless they seek to understand why people stop visiting and why people cross the road to avoid speaking to them, it can lead to deep resentment and anger. This is where the role of support groups becomes important. In the first few days of grief, the thought of joining a group of parents also in loss can seem strange. However, as the weeks pass, parents can find a considerable amount of comfort from being with other parents who understand. Hearing one another's stories can be upsetting, yet it can also reveal that you are not alone and that other people have been where you are and have indeed survived. (Appendix I lists support groups for bereaved parents.)

As the months progress, Christmas comes and goes, the child's birthday passes, and the anniversary of its death approaches. Most parents acknowledge that the fear in anticipating these days proves to be worse than the actual day. It does help to plan such days. You may decide not to celebrate Christmas, or to have only people around you who would not object, regardless of how you feel. You may choose to buy a present for your dead child. On the anniversary of its birth or death you may decide to take a day off work and go into the countryside, to plant a tree, or do some charity work.

Parents, and their friends and relatives tend to assume that after the first anniversary life will suddenly pick up. However, many parents have to brace themselves for a difficult second year. At least in the first year they can recall what they were doing with the child at the same time last year. But the second year of bereavement takes them further away from the events of the past, which parents do not want to leave. Therefore it is important that parents resolve not to drift through another year. They need to decide positively to bring a degree of order and purpose into the home. Small targets can help. It may be:

❤   Working one day a week

❤   Doing some voluntary work

❤   Re-ordering the garden

❤   Taking up writing or painting or pottery

Although parents might not want to carry out any activity, the decision to do so can in itself be therapeutic. This does not mean they will forget the past – how can they when they are thinking about the child constantly? But it does mean they are managing their loss better. Therefore, deciding beforehand what to do when they have a bad day, or when a monthly period arrives, or when the dark nights are depressing, can help to push them through the trough.

It is important, if parents are seeking to have another child, to obtain much support from the doctor, nurses and other carers. Mentally, the more a parent accepts that the next child will be different and unique, with a different name and personality, the more it will assist the whole family. It is sad to see a child grow up totally in the shadow of a deceased brother or sister. It is better to keep cherished photographs and possessions under control and not have them everywhere in the house.

Siblings will still need the support of their parents for years after the death. It helps to be able to talk freely with them about their dead brother or sister, to remember the good times and the difficult times. Parents find it hard to know how to handle their other children after the death of one child. The key is to discuss with the child how parents are feeling; whether about being stricter or more lax, and encourage the child to share its feelings. Children do not always want endless freedom, but will feel more secure if they understand their parents' feelings.

As the years progress, it is helpful for parents to acknowledge positive steps they have taken. The fact that their values in life may have changed needs to be affirmed. In the end, the family that keeps working at communication eventually comes through with the fewest scars. A parent will never forget, but can eventually choose to continue with life – probably in a very different form.

11

How Can Family, Friends and Neighbours Help?

To comfort me, you have to come close.
Come sit beside me on my mourning bench

Nicholas Wolterstorff

When a child dies, it sends a ripple spreading right throughout the community. Apart from people saying,' how awful' and 'why?' they are also asking:

- How do I relate to the child's parents?

- Should I visit?

- Will I send a card or flowers?

- Can I mention the child's name?

- Shall I go to the funeral?

- How can I help?

People have preconceived ideas of what it must be like for the bereaved parents and how they should cope. In reality, we just do not know! It is from this basis of ignorance that we can be of the most help. When we think we understand, the probability is we will misinterpret the situation. When we come to parents, feeling helpless in ourselves but open to helping in any way, then and only then can we be of any assistance.

DOs and DON'Ts

The first thing that many people will do is to send a card of condolence. Please do not underestimate the importance of such cards to parents. Cards where a few words of warm remembrance of the child are written are especially dear to the family. Friends and relatives will also want to telephone or visit the house. Both these actions are very important, and indeed, if they are not carried out, parents will be able to recall the fact years later! It is remarkable how parents cope with visits to the house, provided relatives and friends do not become a burden to the family. It is amazing how often a person visits the bereaved parents and informs them that they can't cope with the news, expecting the parents to care for them! But making this confession can be far better than coming with any preconceived ideas.

When you visit a bereaved parent, please pay attention to this important list of 'do's and don'ts'.

Do **NOT** say:

'Why are you crying?'

'It was worse for Mrs Smith.'

'I understand.'

'Good will come out of it.'

'It was the hospital's fault.'

'He/she is better off dead.'

'He/she has gone to a better place.'

'My divorce was just as painful.'

'Look on the bright side.'

'It could be worse.'

'Call me if you want anything.'

'Try and be wise.'

'I know because I lost my dog.'

'At least he was sixteen.'

'He was just a trouble to you.'

'It will get better.'

'Time heals.'

These are words people have actually said to bereaved parents. If you find that you yourself have said some of them, don't worry, just desire to build afresh.

Things to **DO!**

Listen!

Ask how the child died.

Use the dead child's name.

Seek to empathise rather than sympathise.

Allow parents to react in their own way.

Offer to do specific jobs.

Allow moments of silence.

Recognise that you do not have all the answers.

Allow yourself to be upset, provided you do not burden the family.

In the early days following the child's death, the key role of friends and relatives is to listen over and over again to the story, assuring the bereaved that you love them and are willing to carry out practical jobs, with their permission. There is a great temptation to want to take over when you see people so devastated. However, many parents have told me how resentful they felt when their vulnerability has been used as an excuse for the visitor to take over jobs that parents themselves felt they ought to have done. It can be more helpful to assist the bereaved rather than to dominate. Parents may require assistance with:

❤ Taking children to school, or to the park.

❤ Shopping for food.

❤ Driving them to the funeral director, registry office or mortuary.

❤ Washing or ironing.

❤ Taking care of the pet.

❤ House sitting.

❤ Cutting the grass.

Many people find themselves saying, 'Call me if you want any help.' This is a nice gesture, but don't forget that parents are in a state of confusion and weakness and are therefore probably not able to initiate contact. It is far better to suggest ideas which might help and allow the bereaved to respond as they wish. At a time when parents are extremely distraught, there may be a role for a relative or friend to care for the other children. Friends need to be sensitive in not pushing relatives out, even though the friends may be closer to the parents. It is a delicate task to care for children who themselves are entering grief, often for the first time.

Children observe their parents to see how they should be reacting and behaving. Supremely, they need to grieve with their parents, rather than relatives or friends. Yet parents can find that they are so focused on their loss that they struggle to talk and listen to their other children. Once again, the key role is to listen to children and allow them to say how they are feeling. If the children are asking questions, it is better to say that you do not know the answers than to give them false information which will hinder your relationship with them later on.

It is far better to visit regularly for a few minutes rather than make a long, embarrassing visit which only puts a strain on the family. A short visit, perhaps sitting in silence or crying with the bereaved, can mean infinitely more than trying to justify the whole situation.

When it comes to the funeral, being there at the service provides the biggest support to the family. By making the effort to attend you are communicating so much. The blood relatives tend to play a larger part on the day of the funeral. When relatives return home, they can still prove to be a rich source of help, making regular telephone calls to support the family. A true friend has to be willing to be patient and allow relatives to carry out their duties, knowing that their own support will be called on in time.

What qualities make a good friend at such times? It is common to find that the closest friend of a bereaved parent does not cope with the role easily. Parents probably have friends who themselves have children of the same age. This brings home the insecurity of their own children's lives, to the extent that some friends cannot cope. In the end, the best friend is one who has 'stickability' – the willingness to work at a relationship which cannot be the same as in the past, and in which the friend has to make most, if not all, of the running. If you have this will power over a period of years, you will learn the rest on the job. Clearly, friends who accept the bereaved family as they are, without trying to change them, will prove to be better company for the family. At the end of the day, friends and relatives are on a learning curve of empathy, trying to put themselves into the shoes of the bereaved. This role develops with experience, but there are pointers that are worth noting.

It is helpful to reassure your friend that you are not going to disappear and stop calling as others fall away. You need to decide clearly in your own mind that a difficult visit will not stop you from calling again. If you are rejected, you must try not to take it personally. Ultimately, you can not please the bereaved, for you cannot bring back the one person they want, the deceased child. However, a good friend can be around to listen, and be willing to talk and talk about the child. Parents find the need to keep going over the story of their loss as it is their link with their child. They fear that they may forget. Friends need to be willing to look at photographs and to laugh and cry together. Your aim is to encourage the bereaved to live and cope with today and only today. This may involve sitting with them in silence, without having to fill the vacuum. It may also involve listening to the parents' feelings, their worries, fears and guilt, as well as their dreams. Some days, the bereaved may be extremely downhearted.

If parents acknowledge that they have suicidal thoughts, a friend must be brave enough to talk about their emotions, allowing them to express their pain and heartache. *(See Chapter 13 for more on suicide and depression.)* It is important that friends do not assume a husband and wife are supporting each other – it is common for parents to feel their grief has divided them. Often a bereaved person finds the most support from outside the family. Therefore a friend may be the only person this parent is talking to. Any suicidal tendency needs to be admitted and explored to defuse the situation. Parents often feel better having talked about their negative feelings. As they share with a friend, it may mean the pressure in the marriage is being eased, allowing the bereaved to expect less from their partner because of that support.

Friends can be of invaluable assistance to parents in social situations. They can be within reach if a parent feels trapped in a gathering of people who do not understand, and provide a line of escape when the tension becomes too great. A friend is in a good position to observe when a parent is becoming too dependent on alcohol, or drugs, or to discern when problems are developing in the marriage or with other children. Being truthful with a parent about these issues can help them to stop pretending. Any assistance which encourages a parent to make small steps forward can ultimately transform a situation.

In any pastoral caring role, it is important to acknowledge when you feel a situation is becoming beyond your skill. It is always important to accept within yourself that you have limits. The ability to accept this fact and inform the parent that you feel out of your depth can be the saving of both. There is always someone around who is well qualified to assist if we are willing to turn to them. You may need to encourage the bereaved parent to speak to their doctor, priest, or a support group such as The Compassionate Friends or Cruse.

I want to mention two areas which can be danger points for friends helping bereaved parents. The first is befriending a bereaved parent of the opposite sex. Sympathy, at a time when a person is lost in their own grief, can be misinterpreted. It is far better for people of the same sex to care for each other. Second, I would like to note that friends of the bereaved need care and support also. Friends who take on too much responsibility for caring can find themselves becoming ill, and this can leave them with a sense of guilt for having failed. Anyone caring for a bereaved parent needs to have other channels of support where they can deal with their own guilt and fears.

The good news is that childhood deaths are rarely contagious, therefore as a friend you need not fear, but be assured that you are achieving a great deal as you reach out in love.

Long term caring

As the months and years go by, true friends will remember the child's birthday, and the anniversaries of when the child went into hospital, when the accident occurred, the date of its death and the date of the funeral. It is at such times, as well as in the dark winter nights, that you can be of immense support. Many parents seem to find night time the worst, particularly in winter. A persistent friend or acquaintance, who telephones each week or visits at a regular set time, has proved to be crucial in helping them through a difficult time.

'*My friend would call me each night just as it got dark. She knew this was the worst part of the day for me, as I closed the curtains and felt so isolated and alone.*'

If you can recall the key anniversary dates, then you can be more aware of when the bereaved will need a little more tender loving care.

One place that can be emotionally draining for a parent is the empty bedroom – empty in the sense that the child's physical presence is gone but there remain memories and precious possessions. Friends can play a key role in helping parents cope with this 'special room'. It can seem quite natural to encourage parents to sort out the child's belongings and rearrange the bedroom. However, this can be quite destructive. First, if anyone is to touch the room it is far more therapeutic for parents to carry out the process, however painful. If a friend sorts out the room, parents may later on resent the friend's interference. People may think it is strange to see a parent not altering the bedroom for months or years. Yet for them it is all they have left of their child. These objects are all priceless to a parent:

- The characteristic smell of the room
- The wallpaper, perhaps chosen by the child
- The toys which recall special Christmas events
- The stereo and music that related so well to the mood of the child
- The small possession – watch, ring, necklace, hair brush
- A musical instrument

The best a relative or friend can do, if allowed, is to sit with the parent, surrounded by memories, to allow the parent to speak about their feelings and thoughts of the room, and to recall the happy and difficult times. It is only as parents reveal these thoughts that they can come to a point of tackling the room positively. The outcome for some will be to hold on to a few key possessions and finally to rearrange the room. A friend's role is to help a parent come to a decision that the parent wants, in the parent's timing. To rush the process is to be too detached from the pain of the decision. In the end a person's temperament and personality will dictate the outcome. If a parent decides not to tackle the room, or decides not to move house because of the memories, have we the right to question the decision? Perhaps only if it is preventing the parent from coping with life.

Practical Help

As a caring friend or relative, there are many little roles you can play, which can make all the difference for the bereaved. The aim is to make the bereaved continually feel accepted and wanted:

- Telephone regularly, especially in the winter months, just after it gets dark.

- Send a card or letter at anniversaries, birthdays, Christmas.
  (Do not worry that you will be reminding the parent of the event, they will not have forgotten!)

- Offer to be with them on an anniversary, perhaps taking them out for a drive or walk.

- Offer to help with writing Christmas cards, wrapping presents, etc.
  (It is at a time when people are extremely busy that the bereaved can feel the most alone.)

- Offer to take the other children out somewhere special.

- Send encouraging cards and letters at times other than anniversaries. This can be a real lift.

- Support parents if the wife becomes pregnant, by listening to their hopes and fears.

- Years on, still be willing to remember and talk about the lost child.

As the years slowly go by, parents are not the only ones who need to assess their development. A friend needs to be asking the question, 'How can I continue to support without being trapped?' Ultimately, the fact that you are still around reveals to the bereaved parents that you have achieved something worthwhile. To keep a friendship going through grief requires you to accept the bad days in the relationship and push on to the better days. You will have observed how the past loss creates new worries and fears for the bereaved, whether it is in their marriage, or with other children or with the parents' own health. A listening ear will have been a tremendous help. You will have noticed how the parents' own values in life have changed, and how it has affected your own outlook on life too, hopefully for the better.

Finally, if you do not feel able to live up to such a high calling of friendship, do not lose heart. It takes different levels of friendship if a parent is to move forward in life. They will need friends who pop in less frequently than others. What is important is that you accept your own capability for caring. Some are able to give intensely, while others simply cannot function in this way. This is acceptable. We all carry our own worries, fears and hurts which enable us to care at different levels. It is important that we do not get so involved in caring that we end up neglecting our own marriages and children. We need to be honest with ourselves that we are caring for the right reasons and not running away from our own problems.

Ultimately, any caring is costly and involves a degree of suffering, but the rewards are high in assisting a parent to come through the blackest period of their lives. Years later you may feel you have done little except to be around and willing to listen. If the community fails to recognise this key role, may I on their behalf say 'thank you' – you have achieved much to be proud of.

12

Advice for the Caring Services

The fact of death is so all consuming, you become obsessed by it.

A grieving parent

A t the outset of this chapter, I would like to make it clear to my colleagues in the caring profession that I am not going to 'teach grandma how to suck eggs'. We have all, in our respective professions, received training in caring for people at one level or another. It is not for me to tell you how to carry out your job, but to reflect on my own experience. However, I have listened to parents' and siblings' stories about their bereavement, and it is inevitable that they comment on our professionalism. They view us at times with great admiration, yet at other times with disappointment and excessive anger. None of us will be surprised at this, for we are regularly put in impossible situations which can result only in disappointment. People can so easily look at anyone in authority in a godly way, placing enormous hopes on them. It is therefore understandable that when we do not live up to their false assumptions we receive their anger. Let me therefore draw out a few points for reflection so that as professionals we are at least reviewing our role and our understanding of the needs of the bereaved.

Whether as a doctor, nurse, clergyman or counsellor, society sees us as very much 'in the know'. We are not only supposed to understand the situation that people find themselves in but also to be able to direct them to where they want to be. The average person may know little about medicine, nursing, bereavement, or life after death, but they exist with the conviction that someone does. Yet the reality is that we professionals know so little. Do we really know what it is like to be a parent whose child has been diagnosed with cancer? Even though we have counselled many bereaved people, do we sit where they sit, feeling their pain and suffering? Granted, many counsellors have themselves been bereaved, yet we can so easily fall into the trap of assuming we understand. The fact is, everyone's situation is unique and in any case we can walk away at any point and leave it all behind us. This is both a benefit and a hindrance – a blessing because it is impossible to take on board the weight of people's problems without withdrawing and bringing balance back to our own lives. The hindrance is that we can all too easily be so withdrawn, even in our first encounter with a person, that we do not engage the situation at all!

All workers in the caring professions are seen as miracle workers of some kind. The doctor is the one with the medicine to heal the child. The nurse is encouraged to bring a child through the difficult illness. Before death, the religious minister's prayers are seen as a potential miracle, and even after death he or she is seen as the one with the answers. It is understandable, therefore, that eventually the bereaved can feel let down in their expectations of us all. This is part of the job and we have to acknowledge and accept it. Yet sadly it seems that many professionals at all levels choose not to get too involved in the first place. Thus, when a bereaved parent feels at rock bottom they express their frustration when the professional does not want to share their pain. Can this be changed? I think so, but only if as professionals we have our own support system, which allows us to draw close to those in need, knowing that we ourselves will be cared for when we are feeling drained. I suspect this is where full-time carers are weak. The more experienced we become, the more we can convince ourselves that we can cope alone. The result is that we either break down ourselves or end up withdrawing our 'tender loving care' approach to ministry.

Any support structure for carers needs to take into account our own personalities, skills and stamina, which all affect our particular style of caring. One cannot keep on facing issues of life and death without having this affect our own grief experiences. It is important that we have the opportunity to talk through our own vulnerabilities with a trusted friend. This is especially the case for clergy, who can feel they have no answers to the problems presented to them, yet all around them people are performing practical jobs. We all feel secure when we can give an answer to a question, even if it is the wrong answer. Yet if the clergy's role is to be a 'Christlike figure,' much of our time will be spent attempting to engage the situation without giving quick, false answers.

I recall a time, as hospital Chaplain, when a grandmother angrily picked up her daughter's dead baby and thrust him into my arms, demanding,' Now you tell me why?' Any answer would have been inadequate. My role was to hold the baby and 'be there,' in the painful situation, feeling the pressure of the assault. I was physically, emotionally and spiritually drained as I left the hospital, clearly requiring someone's care, yet I felt I had done nothing. Learning to live in a vulnerable position is very much a part of the job of all carers.

At a time of illness and death, parents assume that a carer will be around long term to support them. This is unrealistic as the full-time worker can only give so much to each situation. Ideally, a local community will provide the on-going support while the professional provides special care at key moments. However, in a society where the community support system is often lacking, great pressures are placed on the full-time worker to be regularly involved. This can ultimately lead to disappointment. Therefore it is better to spell out from the beginning what kind of pastoral support you can provide.

It is the little things the bereaved notice that can hurt the most. When a full time carer forgets the name of the dead child, it can be very upsetting for parents who cannot get the name out of their heads, even if they wanted to. It is a simple job to keep a brief note of such names. It can also be frustrating when a doctor or clergyman just 'pops in for a quick visit'. Obviously, families are pleased we have remembered them but in such short visits a parent or sibling is unlikely to open up and talk about their true feelings. By using simple management skills to organise our busy days, we could allocate the visit an appropriate amount of time. This shows that we are taking their need seriously.

One common factor mentioned by parents is the seeming inability of professionals to be able to direct a bereaved person to an appropriate caring organisation. Granted, the bereaved must initiate the contact with organisations such as Cruse, The Compassionate Friends, SANDS and the National Child Death Helpline themselves, yet it seems that the professionals seldom mention such groups. This leaves bereaved parents in a vacuum, often assuming that no support group exists near them. The ability to refer a bereaved parent to others who can help is surely a sign of a mature professional who knows his or her limitations. It is a simple matter when we visit the bereaved to carry leaflets about the appropriate support groups, leaving it up to the family to initiate contact if they wish.

The medical profession

Doctors can play a key role in assisting the bereaved parents at a time when they may feel their work is complete. Parents do not forget when a doctor fails to visit their home after a child's death. In these early days of grief, the doctor can provide real comfort by visiting and recognising the depth of pain the family feels. It may be a time to give support with tranquillisers, to assist sleep. However, most parents endeavour to do without. In some cases, it seems that tranquillisers are used in a negative way, delaying the grief process a parent needs to go through. But the majority find themselves not requiring such pills weeks or at most a few months after the funeral.

Parents generally appreciate the care that was given by the medical centres which their child attended. Usually, if parents feel that a misdiagnosis of a child's illness took place before its death, they find it easier to move practices, rather than to continue facing the same doctor.

Although families in the early stages of grief seem to show little desire to find a support group or to have counselling, nevertheless the doctor is in a good position at least to provide a leaflet. Weeks or months later, when the doctor has less contact with them and parents are feeling more isolated generally, they feel the need to seek additional support. A leaflet left at the beginning can sow a seed for the future. However, members of several support groups said that medical centres refuse to display notices advertising their existence. The reason given is that it is too negative an image to project to their patients. Surely medical centres are there to care for all aspects of life, which inevitably includes the reality of death and bereavement. The sooner the medical centres break the charade that children do not die, the sooner the local community will be able to face up to and talk more openly about it. Can I therefore encourage everyone to check their medical centre and recommend that it promotes these support groups?

Church involvement

Churches are also involved with the bereaved, both in connection with the funeral and pastoral care afterwards. In a busy job, a minister will generally visit only once after a funeral. After this, contact is lost. Perhaps, in areas where tradition is important, a family may attend Church on the Sunday after the funeral, but unless they are already regular Church goers, probably will not venture into Church again. Many parents tell how upsetting Church services can be, as each hymn reminds them of the funeral and of their child. Yet many parents mentioned that months later, at a time when friends and visitors drop away, they would have valued a pastoral visit from the Church.

Parents can feel extremely guilty about the death of their child, even if in reality they could do nothing to prevent it. The minister can offer help to parents to forgive themselves, whether by absolution or by general counselling. Parents also reach a stage of wanting to know where their child is. Either the child is under the ground and will never be alive again, or in Heaven. If in Heaven, parents want to know whether their son or daughter is growing and changing and, most importantly, whether they will meet again. These are all difficult questions which a parent wants to discuss and reflect upon.

I have already mentioned the danger of a minister jumping in with the hope of resurrection just after the child's death, when parents are unable to relate to the concept. Nevertheless, months later, a minister could prove to be of great assistance by helping the family to work through these questions and formulate at least some answers acceptable to them. To achieve this, churches need to have clear bereavement policies, and perhaps employ the services of a lay worker trained by Cruse to visit the bereaved on behalf of the Church. A regular Service of Remembrance seems to be a comfort to the bereaved, assuring them that they are not forgotten.

From the statistics I have obtained, it is interesting to note that parents generally do not alter their belief concept after the loss of a child, although the degree of intensity may vary. Indeed, as the years of bereavement pass, more parents begin to seek a religious link in the community. This means the churches that maintain pastoral care of the bereaved over years are in a better position to support the parents and help them back into an active community life.

Funeral directors

Funeral directors, like doctors and clergy, are involved with parents at that most painful of times – just after the death of the child. They too can assist with grief management. Funeral directors are called to speak to parents when they are raw and in a state of shock. The more a funeral director can demonstrate his or her own care from a position of deep feeling rather than from a business point of view, the greater will be their assistance to the bereaved. This means, like the clergy, allowing time for the bereaved family to reach decisions. Whether a child should be buried or cremated is too important a consideration to be rushed. A hasty decision by the parents at this stage can lead to long-term regrets. In reality, there are no right or wrong answers. The decisions to be made are ones which the parents feel at peace about. It is the funeral director's role, overlapping with the clergy, to lay out the options before the parents.

Funeral directors, like medical centres, can also provide leaflets about support groups; this demonstrates their sympathy and care. In the end, for all of those in the caring professions, it comes down to whether we are just performing a function or whether we truly want to empathise with those in loss and therefore fulfil a role which, although it may seem small, can make an important difference.

13

Seeking Help . . . and Helping Yourself

At some point there is a moment at which you realise

your child is not coming back

and your original self is never going to be complete or the same.

You will spend the rest of your life living with a major

loss and it is going to be okay. You can do that.

It's not going to be so aching and so terrible that

you can't function, that you can't re-create your own self.

The mother of a teenage accident victim

Tragedy jolts people into taking a deeper look at their lives, their beliefs and their feelings. They gain new insights, but it is sad that tragedy seems to be the only way such different perspectives are reached. We have to acknowledge that some parents become embittered and toughened by the experience. They no longer believe in a just God, or they are angry at the world. They have been scarred for life by the hand of suffering.

Most parents experience nagging fear; the fear that something else awaits them around the corner of life. Such fears gradually decrease over the years, as perhaps their other children grow older and reach a new stage of life which the deceased child never achieved. However, the confidence and innocence of life are somehow never recaptured. We cannot become ourselves again. Yet we can learn to survive, scars and all. Parents are able to carve out a living for themselves as they face the reality of what has happened.

For most parents, there is a change of lifestyle. The loss in pregnancy changes the mother's future perspective. Perhaps she has already given up her job and career because of the expected child. The parents who thought they had achieved their full quiver of children, and have passed on all the baby clothes and children's toys, may find themselves thinking about whether they want to start afresh. Older parents, expecting their child to leave home with a job or a place in college, look forward to having more space and time, but now find they must reassess what they want from their lives. Eventually, for all parents there is the need to rethink their goals, to reorganise their priorities and to move in a new direction. This takes time, patience and courage, for the healing process is extremely slow.

Altruism

Altruism is the practice of unselfish concern for the welfare of others. This is one common factor bereaved parents manifest over time. This action, in whatever form, seems not only to benefit those they care for but also proves to be a strategy that helps the parents to cope themselves.[34] This altruistic behaviour may take a variety of forms:

- Joining support groups

- Supporting local hospitals

- Raising finance for charities

- Drawing attention to specific illnesses and diseases

- Initiating a charity

- Writing a book about their experiences

- Having another child

It may seem strange to have the birth of a baby on this list. However this provides the parent with an opportunity to fulfil altruism in its ultimate form: the giving of oneself totally to another child.

In most of these cases, the parents find themselves replacing the role of parenting with another lesser, yet relevant, role. This is indeed a sign of some form of successful resolution of grief. As the bereaved reinvest their love and energy into another object, it provides a form of comfort and adds purpose to their lives. When this does occur, there is evidence that it reduces the degree or likelihood of depression.[35]

The ability of a parent to seek out a support group after months of bereavement is in fact an important sign of what is going on in them. It shows the desire to begin to tackle their situation in a positive way. Naturally, bereaved parents' personalities vary, and therefore the degree of altruism varies in accordance with the nature of the individual. As the years progress, this intensity of outward care diminishes, although it seems that bereaved parents remain more altruistic than the general public.

Support groups

How do parents begin to gather up the pieces of their lives and cope with the nagging memories so that they can concentrate afresh on other activities? Sometimes their family and friends are just not enough. Parents resort to seeking out others in similar situations so that there might be a common ground of empathy and understanding. By sharing their emotions with those in a similar position they can believe that their own reactions are normal. Here, parents discover that they are not going crazy:

---

[34]L Videka-Sherman, 'Coping with the Death of a Child', *American Journal of Orthopsychiatry*, 1982, Vol 52.

[35]T Rando, 'Bereaved Pareants: Particular Difficulties, Unique Factors and Treatment Used', *Social Work*, 1985.

'To hear that I wasn't the only one to break every ornament in my house was such a relief.'

There seems to come a time when a bereaved person feels able to cope with joining such a group. In the early weeks of loss, parents are just too raw in pain to join anything, but after a few months, when the support and interest of others has decreased, parents seem to be looking for extra support. Such groups are therapeutic when one partner in a marriage wants to talk about the loss but the other partner refuses.

Support groups encourage altruistic behaviour. They offer a forum for parents to express their own views with confidence that people in the group will understand. Members are encouraged not only to share themselves but also to care for other members in similar situations. This leads to the therapeutic effect of gently shifting the bereaved parents' preoccupation from themselves to the care of others.[36]

Initially, there is a variety of reasons for attending such groups, but often it reveals inadequate care support by the wider community. In the intensity of bereavement, family support is not enough for an individual. This does not necessarily mean the family has failed, but reveals the complex nature of what occurs in a family group. When those you normally turn to are in bereavement themselves, it is understandable that you may need others for support. However, it does seem that fathers are less likely to join such groups, preferring to keep their feelings to themselves.

This can cause tension in some families, if one or more members actively discourage involvement in a support group. Initially, the step of attending a group can seem to be an enormous mountain to climb. It may be the first time a parent has told the story of the child's death to a small anonymous group. Yet, if the leader of a group visits the parent first, fears can be put at ease sufficiently to allow the parent to give it a go. I think this reveals the depth of pain a bereaved parent must be experiencing, to open themselves up to a group. Yet, for many it can be a lifeline that sees them through a difficult period of their loss.[37]

'My friends think it sounds awful, sitting around sharing our stories. They think it keeps bringing the event back to me. But how can it, for it never goes away'

'I feel at ease there because no one ever says, "pull yourself together" or asks "why are you crying?"'

'Here, I could talk without people backing off. They want to listen.'

It seems the key to success in such groups is not so much what the group members do for each other, but that rather what the individuals begin to do for themselves. Here the bereaved parent learns to share and to listen in a safe environment. This proves to be a catalyst for the individual to begin to see others around them who not only understand but want to help. Gradually, the parents find themselves helping new members of the group in a way that takes them out of themselves productively.

---

[36]L Videka Sherman, *op cit.*

[37]D Klass, 'Bereaved parents and The Compassionate Friends: Affiliation and Healing', *Omega*, 1984-5, Vol 15 (4).

On the negative side, some parents can eventually feel trapped in self-help groups, whether as a leader or just as a member. Some feel the group was helpful at first, but in time prevented them from moving forward in life. Continually telling their story in a group makes them dwell on the past perhaps more than they wish.

> *'At first the group was a great help. But now I worry that some just have not moved on in their grief. Because they support me, I feel I have to go on supporting them. I feel trapped, so that if I stopped going I would be letting the side down, rather like a caravan club.'*

One mother, six months after the death of her husband, had joined a bereavement group set up by the local GP clinic. Her reaction to this group highlights the dangers of classification.

> *'I'm leaving the group as I feel I don't give the standard answers the counsellor is expecting from me. I want to be able to be myself rather than feel I must jump through expected hoops of some bereavement process.'* [38]

The groups can also appeal specifically to those from a middle class background, who may be more familiar with group dynamics. However, on the whole, the groups generally seem to enable individuals to help themselves. Provided the group has a process for letting go of members, then undoubtedly they perform a service that the community desperately needs.

Having more children

One way that parents perform the role of altruism is by having another child, whether naturally or by adoption. In reality, of course it is impossible for any new child to be a replacement for another. Yet this is exactly the expectation that communities place on many parents. The danger of this is that it does not take seriously the impact of the first child. Having another child too quickly allows no time for a parent to mourn the loss of the child who died. This can lead to a confusion of emotions, for the parent and eventually for the second child. The parent may not be physically ready to give birth again, thus leading to exhaustion later on. Also, emotions can easily take over. A mother and father can find themselves attempting to love their second child, at the same time deeply mourning the loss of their first. This can cause them to make wrong projections on the living child.

Parents can find that the second child is just never good enough. The imagination can run wild, with a parent believing that the deceased child would have been perfect and not have made the mistakes that their existing child makes. Somehow, the living child never comes up to scratch. Sometimes a parent calls the second child by the first child's name. This can create a poor self-image in the living child and make it confused about who it is meant to be. The child grows up in a world surrounded by the 'perfect child.' The new child may have to sleep in the deceased child's bedroom, and have to share the living room with several photographs of their dead brother or

---

[38]Personal interview.

sister. They may start to feel that another is cherished more than they are. The child grows up with a model of 'not being present,' and can therefore become distant to his or her parents.[39] The child also silently carries the fear that it too will die young.

In some families, problems result not necessarily from having the second child so soon after bereavement but rather from how to bring up the second child. Should they be extra protective, so as to make sure that this child does not die? Or more lenient, for fear of upsetting the child? If a child is brought up at one extreme or the other, there are frequently problems later, in adolescence. Perhaps the common factor in all of these circumstances is communication. The more a couple are able to talk through their grief and discuss their feelings about their children, the less the chance of problems. This is true too for the children; they also need to be involved in discussion about their dead brother or sister and how they feel in regard to their upbringing. It is not uncommon for a child greatly to resent the deceased child as an intrusion upon their lives, with parents never realising this. Children need to be valued for themselves, irrespective of other siblings.

There are, of course, positive sides to having more children after a bereavement. It gives a chance for a family to begin to build afresh and to look forward with new hope. Of course there will be worrying moments, yet the rewards will outweigh the tensions, provided the family pull together. It is here that parents will also need the support of family and friends, as they bravely enter into pregnancy once again. They will also need the support of a caring doctor to provide the medical assurance that is needed.

Older parents, who are unable to start a family afresh suffer deep scars, as already mentioned. Not only is the past wiped out for them, but also the future is bereft of all hope. The road to recovery, gaining new hopes and desires, is harder to find. The need to find self-worth in such cases frequently leads to altruistic behaviour – helping others, whether it be in the family or outside in the community.

Depression and Suicide

An important similarity that appears to be characteristic of parents who have suffered the loss of a child – at whatever age and for what ever reason – is the contemplation of their own death as a way of legitimising the loss. Child death seems so inappropriate, unnatural and unacceptable in our modern society that it is not fully comprehended. This is true where the death is sudden and unexpected. There is no context into which such an event can be fitted. Consequently, it appears to many parents – especially mothers, but fathers too – that survival for themselves is at best questionable. There appears to be no hope, no way of justifying their lives, no way of continuing with life without the deceased child. Many parents therefore come to the point where they

---

[39]C Legg and I Sherick, 'The Replacement Child', *Psychiatry and Human Development*, 1976, Vo. 7.

sincerely want to die themselves; to follow their child to the grave in a blind but understandable desire to continue to see, caress and love it. Along with this, there is also an intense desire to escape the pain of separation. The devastation and agony that they feel almost drive them into suicide. And this experience is not just short-lived. Many parents interviewed said that they still had remnants of their desire to end it all several years after the loss.

There are two phases at work in this aspect of loss. First, there is the acute phase – feelings of desolation and wanting to escape from life. The bereaved parent can teeter on the brink of self-destruction for anything from two weeks to three months.[40] The chronic phase is much longer, but is characterised by less intense feelings. In my own interviewing, I found that this chronic phase lasts much longer than many realise. Where a mother still wants to end it all three or five years on, yet friends and relatives prefer not to talk about the past any longer, there is clearly an area of great stress. This chronic phase, I suggest, lasts for at least three years, after which it gradually subsides, but never fully disappears. Parents' reactions here are 'take it or leave it'. They tend to have no overt fear of death in any form and even though they may no longer contemplate taking their lives, they would still consider allowing death to occur.

A large dose of anger is very much present here, often directed at the deceased. This in turn creates guilt and more despondency. One mother believed that her anger was projected irrationally at her surviving daughter.

'I started to pick on my daughter; why wasn't it her instead of my son?'

For the majority, a plateau is reached in which the parent copes on a daily basis.

'Some days you wake up and just know it's going to be a black day. The only way through it is that I tell myself, it's like the weather, it will pass even if it will come again.'

Suicidal tendencies can remain high on the agenda of a parent if there are other factors restricting the degree of recovery taking place. For example, one mother reached a suicidal breaking point because of the way her husband was treating her.

'He made me feel worthless because he ignored my feelings, my child's birthday, anniversaries and photos.'

Full nervous breakdowns requiring medical assistance can occur. I have found that fathers as well as mothers experience this, between two and three years after the death. This delay challenges the concept that parents are starting to recover between twelve and eighteen months after the death of a child. This also seemed to occur regardless of the age of the child. When plunged into a pit of intense despair and depression, it is certainly clear that parents lose their zest for living. However, when society ignores this crying gap in one's life, some oblige society and wear the mask which says everything is okay, whether at work or at home. The majority of parents seem to plod on with a kind of mundane existence, exhibiting a decrease in motivation and deterioration in their own health. Many, particularly the mothers of older children, never seem to regain the

---

[40]R Knapp, *Beyond Endurance, op cit.*

energy to motivate themselves, preferring to sit quietly and watch the world go by without participating. It has been suggested that the impact on some individuals is so great that the brain undergoes physical changes that prevent recovery. However, data to support this theory is lacking.

Many parents, however, do find a turning point at which they begin to live life afresh. One key factor in this is other children. If it is the oldest child who dies, usually the younger children in the family keep the parents looking forward. However, when the youngest at home is taken from a family, parents have far less to jolt them from their depression.

'I had become addicted to sherry and was becoming very suicidal. It was when I felt my deceased son say to me, "Mum, what are you doing?" that I turned around.'

One mother had only recently been divorced before her daughter's death. The feelings of depression and suicidal thoughts she had experienced in the divorce enabled her to acknowledge that suicide wasn't the answer.

One motivating factor which helps parents to keep going is the recognition that their own death would probably compound the hurt already experienced by other family members. They may prefer death, but at the same time they recognise their responsibilities to others. So they hang on to life and hope for the best. Positive things can come out of such suicidal feelings. A mother whose son had committed suicide said:

'I now understand my son who committed suicide, there is a very thin line between doing it or not.'

Others reveal that it is only when they finally reach the very bottom that they are able to begin to progress. Here an attitude of will plays an important part. Those who desire to progress and move on in life eventually achieve their desires. It is worth noting that, with every couple I interviewed, one or other of the parents felt so emotional that they cried. This was not just a mother's reaction: in most cases the father also showed signs of tears. There was no correlation either with the period since the child's death or whether they had lost a baby, child or young person. In all cases, visible emotions were aroused by the simple questions addressed to them about their bereavement. This highlights the depth of pain which occurs with such tragedies. There was also a positive reaction, even in tears. Although they were not looking forward to the interview, they were pleased to talk about their child. It is clear that however many years have passed, parents still want to talk about their child.

It seems that the more a bereaved parent has someone who is willing to listen to them, without judgement, the less their degree of depression. The experience of deep ongoing depression and suicidal tendencies will decrease, the more attention, affection, approval and comfort the bereaved receive. Mourners need a friend and companion who will journey with them through their grief, helping them eventually to live with the loss as well as appreciate the present. However, if the bereaved parent continues, over years, to feel neglected, rejected and generally uncared for, then it is more likely to lead to disastrous thinking. A sense that they do not matter to anyone, which in itself leads to anxiety and deepening hurt, will result in unhealthy behaviour, with a painful outcome.

Letting go

As this book has shown, the road to recovery is a long one for bereaved parents and their children. It is a road that they never thought they would be on and they often find no one else travelling their way. No wonder, therefore, that it leads to such enormous changes in people's lives that they are never the same again. Society seems to suggest that time will heal. Indeed, they seem to expect this healing to be achieved quickly and without too much change, either for the parents or for themselves. This is just not the case. Time provides a backcloth for healing only if the bereaved are willing and able, with support, to tackle their pain and loss.

The parents' trust in so many things has been destroyed. The trust that children will always be around is gone. The trust that one's partner and family will understand is clouded. The trust that friends and neighbours care is challenged. The trust that medicine and God will come to the rescue vanishes in smoke. What is left is the will to go on and sustain one's existence. However weak that seed is in a parent, nevertheless, in the majority, it begins to grow.

Parents slowly begin to trust afresh, within their circle of family and friends. Reconciliation occurs with those around who never really understood what the parents had been through. The relationships may not be the same, but at least they begin an element of dialogue. However, the bereaved parents' perspective of life is radically different from before. Now, they are far more aware of the presence of death around them. They spend their time doing far more what they want to do, rather than following the crowd. They suffer fools less gladly than before. Gradually, positive growth does take place in their lives and they do recognise this. Generally, the parents become less career-conscious and less materialistic. They become more compassionate with others in loss, and more altruistic.

'We were always planning for a rainy day . . . now we simply live day by day. It's all that matters.'

'When people were off work with illness or bereavement I had little sympathy with them, but now I'd do anything to help them.'

Inevitably, the whole process of bereavement ages the parents. Many have shared with me that they still, after eight, ten or twelve years, think constantly about their child. Some are still unable to see anything good resulting from the loss.

'It ruins your life, and even though it is common, that doesn't help.'

'No, I can't see anything good resulting from this, it never gets better. I just cope with it, time doesn't heal.' (A mother after eight years of bereavement)

Perhaps we should not be surprised at such a comment, for the life of a child goes deep within a mother or father. Granted, we live in a world where there is atrocious abuse of children; nevertheless the majority of parents care deeply for their children. One sign of our love and care for our children is that we are willing to suffer for them. For the majority of parents, the degree of suffering is usually only tested with demands on time and finance. However, bereaved parents suffer in a far deeper way. If they love their children, then to be without them is an ongoing suffering. To think constantly about the one you now can never have is torture. To let go of the pain is almost to admit that you do not care any longer. Parents are therefore in the dilemma of wanting to get on with their lives without letting go of the deceased child. The majority of parents continue in this 'suffering love' throughout their lives. They suffer because they love, a love that they are not willing to surrender.

For most, this means reaching a point in their lives where they can enjoy each day afresh, even though they are carrying a wound within them that can never be healed, this side of life.

14

Assessing Your Own Progress

Life may be understood looking backward,
but life must be lived looking forward.

Anonymous

There comes a point in bereaved parents' lives when they want to move forward. It is common for parents to say they wish that they were feeling better after the first few months of bereavement, only to discover that the process takes much longer than they expected. Often, it is relatives and friends who notice a difference in parents as they begin to recover, long before the parents observe it themselves. This is understandable, as parents have moments each day of recalling their loved one which overshadow them, yet that does not mean they do not have good periods as well.

One way of observing progress is for parents to make notes of how they are feeling. As the months and years go by, it is helpful to observe how the notes taken have changed in intensity. Some find it helpful to write letters to their dead child or to express their feelings in poetry or pictures.

Clearly, a parent's progress through bereavement will depend on several factors:

- ♥ The type of relationship the parent had with the deceased.

- ♥ The type of death the child experienced.

- ♥ The type of support available

- ♥ Previous unresolved losses of loved ones

- ♥ Stress factors such as divorce, loss of a job, illness

- ♥ Factors such as religion, age of the parent, personal characteristics

At first, remembering every detail of the loss is important, but when parents eventually realise that they will not lose the memory, this becomes less significant. Making a list of positive things they achieved for their child can bring some reassurance for those who have lost older children. Another motivating factor is to ask the question, 'What would my child have wanted me to now do?' Clearly, parents can not be bound by the child, yet this can initially prove to be a good catalyst.

The questions which follow are intended to provide parents with a way to express how they feel at a various stages of their bereavement. There are no right or wrong answers. If you ask yourself these questions regularly over a period of time, I hope you will begin to see differences in your behaviour and attitudes. There will be some answers that change very quickly, whereas it may take years for others to alter, and a few will perhaps remain constant. I suggest that the first time you look at the questions, simply answer them spontaneously and then put the answers away without any further consideration or study. The answers will only become relevant the second or third time you complete the form. Then you can begin to compare them with your previous responses. If you find that there are questions which cause deep disturbance over time, this can be a sign that you would benefit from talking the issue over with a friend or a counsellor.

Assessing your own progress

I think about my dead child.

Date	Often	Sometimes	Rarely
Date	Often	Sometimes	Rarely
Date	Often	Sometimes	Rarely

I am mixing with people in social situations.

Date	Often	Sometimes	Rarely
Date	Often	Sometimes	Rarely
Date	Often	Sometimes	Rarely

I can talk about my child without undue emotion or pain

Date	Often	Sometimes	Rarely
Date	Often	Sometimes	Rarely
Date	Often	Sometimes	Rarely

I use present/past tense when talking about my child.

Date	Present	Past
Date	Present	Past
Date	Present	Past

I can concentrate on a task at hand.

Date	Often	Sometimes	Rarely
Date	Often	Sometimes	Rarely
Date	Often	Sometimes	Rarely

I dream about my child.

Date	Often	Sometimes	Rarely
Date	Often	Sometimes	Rarely
Date	Often	Sometimes	Rarely

I can enjoy close relationships with other people.

Date	Often	Sometimes	Rarely
Date	Often	Sometimes	Rarely
Date	Often	Sometimes	Rarely

I am interested in other things and people.

Date	Often	Sometimes	Rarely
Date	Often	Sometimes	Rarely
Date	Often	Sometimes	Rarely

I am able to smile and laugh without feeling guilty.

Date	Often	Sometimes	Rarely
Date	Often	Sometimes	Rarely
Date		Often	Sometimes	Rarely

I am over eating/drinking.

Date	Often	Sometimes	Rarely
Date	Often	Sometimes	Rarely
Date	Often	Sometimes	Rarely

I am accident prone.

Date	Often	Sometimes	Rarely
Date	Often	Sometimes	Rarely
Date	Often	Sometimes	Rarely

I am ill with minor ailments.

Date	Often	Sometimes	Rarely
Date	Often	Sometimes	Rarely
Date	Often	Sometimes	Rarely

I am irritated with my family relationships.

Date	Often	Sometimes	Rarely
Date	Often	Sometimes	Rarely
Date	Often	Sometimes	Rarely

I feel a burden on others.

Date	Often	Sometimes	Rarely
Date	Often	Sometimes	Rarely
Date	Often	Sometimes	Rarely

I fantasise about suicide.

Date	Often	Sometimes	Rarely
Date	Often	Sometimes	Rarely
Date	Often	Sometimes	Rarely

I resent other people's happiness.

Date	Often	Sometimes	Rarely
Date	Often	Sometimes	Rarely
Date	Often	Sometimes	Rarely

I feel guilty.

Date	Often	Sometimes	Rarely
Date	Often	Sometimes	Rarely
Date	Often	Sometimes	Rarely

I feel angry.

Date	Often	Sometimes	Rarely
Date	Often	Sometimes	Rarely
Date	Often	Sometimes	Rarely

I am unable to sleep.

Date	Often	Sometimes	Rarely
Date	Often	Sometimes	Rarely
Date	Often	Sometimes	Rarely

I have let go of my child's possessions.

Date	None	Some	Most
Date	None	Some	Most
Date	None	Some	Most

I have altered my child's bedroom.

Date	Not at all	A bit	Completely
Date	Not at all	A bit	Completely
Date	Not at all	A bit	Completely

I can look at photographs with joy.

Date	Often	Sometimes	Rarely
Date	Often	Sometimes	Rarely
Date	Often	Sometimes	Rarely

I can see positive things resulting from the death.

Date	None	A few	More
Date	None	A few	More
Date	None	A few	More

I visit the doctor.

Date	Often	Sometimes	Rarely
Date	Often	Sometimes	Rarely
Date	Often	Sometimes	Rarely

I am using sleeping pills / tranquillisers.

Date	Often	Sometimes	Rarely
Date	Often	Sometimes	Rarely
Date	Often	Sometimes	Rarely

I have joined a support group.

Date	No	Considering it	Yes
Date	No	Considering it	Yes
Date	No	Considering it	Yes

I have helped to raise finance for charities.

Date	No	Considering it	Yes
Date	No	Considering it	Yes
Date	No	Considering it	Yes

I support others in bereavement.

Date	Often	Sometimes	Rarely
Date	Often	Sometimes	Rarely
Date	Often	Sometimes	Rarely

I dread the anniversary of my child's death.

Date	Often	Sometimes	Rarely
Date	Often	Sometimes	Rarely
Date	Often	Sometimes	Rarely

I enjoyed last Christmas.

Date	No	A bit	Yes
Date	No	A bit	Yes
Date	No	A bit	Yes

I visit the graveside.

Date	Often	Sometimes	Rarely
Date	Often	Sometimes	Rarely
Date	Often	Sometimes	Rarely

I keep going over and over the events.

Date	Often	Sometimes	Rarely
Date	Often	Sometimes	Rarely
Date	Often	Sometimes	Rarely

I have bought new clothes for myself.

Date	No	Considering it	Yes
Date	No	Considering it	Yes
Date	No	Considering it	Yes

I spend time in my child's room.

Date	Often	Sometimes	Rarely
Date	Often	Sometimes	Rarely
Date	Often	Sometimes	Rarely

I am back at work full time.

Date	No	Part Time	Yes
Date	No	Part Time	Yes
Date	No	Part Time	Yes

I feel upset having looked at these questions.

Date	Yes	A bit	No
Date	Yes	A bit	No
Date	Yes	A bit	No

I feel as if I have come through grief.

Date	Rarely	Sometimes	Often
Date	Rarely	Sometimes	Often
Date	Rarely	Sometimes	Often

Please note again that there are no correct answers, just the recognition of how you are feeling and perceiving things at the present time. All of these questions are about things which can come up in a natural conversation with a friend who is willing to listen and care.

Appendix I

Organisations and Resources

The Compassionate Friends
53 North Street
Bristol
BS3 1EN
Helpline: **0117-953-9639**

A society of parents who have themselves experienced the loss of a child which seeks to help and support those whose children have died at any age.

Cot Death Support Group
14 Halkin Street,
London, SW1 7DP
Tel. 0181 882 4363
24 hour help line
Telephone: **0171 235 1721**

This group undertakes study and research as well as providing information on local self-support groups.

Cruse – Bereavement Care
126 Sheen Road,
Richmond, Surrey
TW9 1UR
Telephone: **0181-332-7227**

The national association for those who are bereaved. They have local branches which offer counselling and practical advice.

National Child Death Helpline
Freephone: **0800-282986**
Daily from 7pm to 10pm
Wednesdays from 10am to 1pm

A telephone helpline especially for anyone affected by the death of a child, not only parents, but grandparents, siblings, teachers, and friends.

The Samaritans
See local Telephone Directories.

Volunteers who provide a telephone listening system 24 hours a day.

Stillbirth and Neo-Natal Death Society (SANDS)
Portland Place,
London W1N 4DE
Telephone: **0171-436-5881**

Supports families whose children have been stillborn or who have died in infancy. They run local self-help groups throughout the country.

Support After Termination For Abnormality (SATFA)
Charlotte Street,
London
W1P 1LB
Telephone: **0171-631-0285**

Supports parents through ante-natal screening and diagnosis. They provide ongoing support to parents who decide to terminate a pregnancy because an abnormality has been detected.

Points for Reflection

His little arms crept round my neck

And then I heard him say

Four simple words I shan't forget

Words that made me pray

They turned a mirror on my soul

And secrets no one knew

They startled me, I hear them yet

He said, 'I'll be like you.'

Herbert Parker

These questions are intended to help people in the caring professions to consider in advance how they might help bereaved parents to understand and deal with their grief, pain, guilt, anger and fear. They are also useful discussion questions for anyone involved in bereavement counselling or in training bereavement counsellors.

Miscarriage, stillbirth, cot death

1. *Imagine you are the neighbour of a couple who are returning home without their baby. How would you feel about visiting them?*

2. *A mother has a baby diagnosed with a genetic disorder which will result in death before the child is four years old. The mother is a professional child minder. What reactions and problems do you envisage developing for this mother in relation to her friends and her work?*

3. *In pregnancy classes, should prospective parents be told of the risks of a typical delivery of a baby?*

4. *Having lost a baby two years previously, you now have a healthy baby girl. When asked months later how many children you have, what do you reply?*

5. *What is the dilemma for parents if they are asked whether they want an autopsy of their deceased child?*

6. *Your eight year old son would like to see his baby brother who died at birth. The baby has a deformed backbone. What are the reasons for and against your son seeing his brother?*

7. *Alice is about to give birth to her second child, having lost her first child through cot death syndrome. Alice would like a night monitor and weighing scales to assess her new baby's development, whereas her husband would prefer not to have any assistance. What are the pros and cons in such a decision?*

8. *A recent report suggests that cot death syndrome can be prevented by sleeping the baby on its back. How would you feel if your child died of cot death syndrome while lying on its tummy?*

Childhood death

1. *What are the key factors to consider in telling a child he or she may not recover from the illness?*

2. *Your child has developed a cyst on his arm. The doctor tells you he can deal with it and will see you again in four weeks. What are the questions revolving around in your head?*

3. *Parents are told that their daughter has a tumour. They are encouraged to keep the situation confidential initially. In what way will the parents find this suggestion difficult?*

4. *A mother has stopped work to care for her dying child. The husband is under pressure in his own job and returns home each night at 7pm. What are the expectations of a mother and father in such a situation?*

5. *It is now three years since your friend lost her nine year old son. How do you feel about mentioning his name?*

6. *When a child is terminally ill, should a parent change the way he or she disciplines the child?*

7. *Why do parents often keep their children away from a terminally ill child even when they know that the illness is not contagious?*

Teenagers

1. *How do you think family relationships change when parents discover their teenage son has a terminal illness?*

2. *When a teenager has died in the parents' home, what are the issues involved in moving from that house?*

3. *Can anything beneficial result from the fact that a teenager ends up in a coma for two weeks before dying after a car accident?*

4. *In what ways do you think a family can deal with guilt when their teenage daughter dies suddenly?*

5. *What would you say to a friend who tells you she feels so angry with her son who died in a motor bike accident?*

6. *Imagine the reactions you might experience reading a deceased teenager's diary for the first time.*

Young adults

1. *Imagine what types of hopes and expectations parents develop in regard to their adult working children?*

2. *In what ways is bereavement different when a son or daughter dies having lived away from home for several years, compared with the loss of a child still living at home?*

3. *How long would you expect a parent to take in getting back to normal life after the death of their twenty-year-old son?*

4. *Your twenty-three year old son has been killed in a traffic accident. There seems to be evidence that the Highway Authority was negligent. What are the reasons for pursuing a claim as compared to letting it pass?*

5. *What emotions might surface for parents who receive money resulting from the death of their adult child?*

6. *In what ways does a bereaved husband or wife have a complex relationship with their parents in-law?*

Common patterns in grief

1. *How do you think the events just before a death affect the parents' grief long term?*
2. *Think through a parent's reactions when a child goes into remission having previously been diagnosed as terminally ill.*
3. *Imagine you are a nurse asking parents of a dead teenager whether their child carried a donor card. What would be your fears?*
4. *Why do you think parents find it easier to look at photographs rather than a video of their dead child?*
5. *Why do many parents feel refreshed having dreamed about their lost child?*
6. *What are the dangers of sorting out a child's bedroom too quickly?*
7. *Why do you think friends and relatives find it harder than parents to talk about a deceased child several years after the death?*

Personal networks

1. *In what ways do you think a husband and wife might try and support each other through a time of grief?*
2. *In a family of four children, when one of the children dies how do you imagine your relationship might change with the remaining children? Over the first few weeks? A year later?*
3. *What extra problems might develop when a couple have previously been divorced before their child dies?*
4. *How can relatives and friends care for siblings when the parents are in a state of grief?*
5. *What factors should be considered in telling siblings what is happening to their ill brother or sister?*
6. *What are the pros and cons of siblings seeing the deceased brother or sister?*
7. *How might you support a grandparent who has lost a grandchild?*

The funeral

1. *Imagine your friend's child has died unexpectedly. Think through what words you would use on a condolence card.*
2. *From the funeral services you have attended, what part of the service remains prominent in your mind?*
3. *How important is it that siblings are given the opportunity to attend the funeral?*
4. *What factors play a part in whether or not a person decides to visit a deceased child in the Chapel of Rest?*
5. *What are the reasons for and against burial or cremation of a baby or child?*
6. *What role can doctors, nurses, etc. play in helping bereaved parents at the time of a funeral?*

Role of religion

1. *Recall a difficult moment in your life. In what ways did others help you through such a time?*
2. *What parts of the Bible relate to childhood deaths?*
3. *What answer would you give a parent who asks, 'Where do you think my dead child is now?'*
4. *How would you expect grieving parents to react to the concept of the Resurrection? two weeks after the death? two years later?*

How can parents and siblings cope?

1. *Would you imagine your closest relationship becoming stronger or weaker because of a death in the family?*
2. *Imagine you are first on the scene at a friend's house where parents have just discovered their child dead in the bathroom. What would you do?*
3. *Imagine your sister has just lost a child. You, however, live in another country. In what ways can you help?*
4. *How can a parent help children at 4, 8, 12, and 17 years of age to begin to face the concept of death?*
5. *Write your own funeral service, and leave clear notes of your wishes in a sealed envelope with your will or your private belongings.*

Relatives, friends and neighbours

1. *Why do you think people cross the road to avoid a recently bereaved person?*
2. *Why is it that we feel awkward when sitting in silence with a person?*
3. *In what ways might a friend be supportive to a bereaved parent over several years?*
4. *How would you feel, as a close relative of the dead child, observing its parents' friends carrying out a key role in the home?*
5. *In what ways can a young friend of the deceased child help the bereaved parents?*
6. *How can helping the bereaved parents both assist and hinder your own life?*

Professionals

1. *How does the fact that, as professionals, we can leave a situation behind hinder us in our ministry?*
2. *How can we handle our own emotions so that we do not become hardened and distant to our patients?*
3. *What structures can we set in place to enable us to assess how we are relating to people?*
4. *In what ways can medical centres, Churches, and funeral homes provide a more comprehensive care structure?*
5. *How can the professional bodies, doctors, clergy, funeral directors and counsellors, relate more fully to each other without breaking the code of confidentiality?*

Seeking help and helping yourself

1. *Why does altruism prove to be such a good 'healer'?*
2. *What should be the main qualities of a support group?*
3. *Why do some families and friends resent support groups?*
4. *How can family and friends advise correctly with regard to bereaved parents having more children?*
5. *How and when should parents talk to their remaining children about the deceased child?*
6. *If a friend is showing signs of depression, how would you help?*
7. *What do you think are the signs that a bereaved person has reached the point of living life 'normally' again ?*

Appendix III

Further Reading

Many of the authors listed have also published other works relevant to the subject.

Ainsworth-Smith, I, *Letting Go*, SPCK, London, 1982.

Bluebond-Langner, M, *The Private Worlds of Dying Children*, New Jersey, 1978.

Borg, S, *When Pregnancy Fails*, Routledge & Keegan, London, 1982.

Campbell, A, *Rediscovering Pastoral Care*, Darton, Longman and Todd, London, 1981.

Donnelly, K, *Recovering from the Loss of a Child*, Macmillan, London, 1982.

Dyregrov, A, and Matthisen, S, 'Parental grief following the death of an infant', *Scandinavian Journal of Psychology*, 1991, Vol. 32.

Giesbrecht, P, *Where is God when a Child Suffers?* Hannibal, Hannibal, 1988.

Glick, I, et al, *The First Year of Bereavement*, John Wiley & Sons, New York, 1974.

Hauerwas, S, *Naming the Silences*, Eerdmans, Michigan, 1990.

Knapp, R, *Beyond Endurance*, Schochen, New York, 1986.

Koocher, G P, & O'Malley, J E, *The Damocles Syndrome*, McGraw-Hill, London, 1981.

Krementz, J, *How It Feels when a Child Dies*, Victor Gollanz, London, 1983.

Kübler-Ross, E, *On Death & Dying*, Tavistock, London, 1970.

Kübler-Ross, E, *On Children and Death*, Macmillan, New York, 1983.

Kushner, H, *When Bad Things Happen to Good People*, Pan, London, 1981.

Merrington, B, *Bereavement in Families*, MPh Thesis, Birmingham University, 1995.

Neubauer, R, Association for Mariage and Family Therapy, New York, quoted in Donnelly, K, *Recovering from the Loss of a Child*, Macmillan, London, 1982.

Payne, J, et al, Psychosocial Adjustment of Families Following the Death of a Child, in *The Child with Cancer*, Thomas, Springfield, Illinois, 1980.

Ponzetti, J, 'The Forgotten Grievers', *Death Studies*, 1991.

Rando, T, 'An Investigation of Grief and Adaption In Parents whose Children have Died from Cancer', *Journal of Paediatric Psychology*, 1983, Vol.8.

Raphael, B, *The Anatomy of Bereavement*, Basic Books, New York, 1983.

Richardson, J, *A Death in the Family*, Lion Publishing, Oxford, 1979

Roskin, M, 'Emotional Reaction among Bereaved Israeli Parents', *Israeli Journal of Psychiatry & Related Sciences*, 1984, Vol. 21, No.2.

Sanders, C, 'A Comparison of Adult Bereavement in the Death of a Spouse, Child and Parent', *Omega*, 1979, Vol. 10.

Sanders, J, *Facing Loneliness*, Highland, Crowborough, 1988.

Schiff, H S, ed, *The Bereaved Parent*, Crown Publishers, New York, 1977.

Schowalter, J, et al, *The Child and Death.*, Culumbria, New York, 1983.

Spinetta, J, et al, 'Effective Parental Coping Following the Death of a Child From Cancer', *Journal of Paediatric Psychology*, 1981, Vol. 6, No.3.

Staudacher, C, *Beyond Grief*, New Harbinger, 1987.

Surin, K, *Theology and the Problem of Evil*, Blackwell, London, 1986.

Tatlebaum, J, *The Courage To Grieve: Creative Living, Recovery & Growth*, Lippincot & Crowell, New York, 1980.

Valeriote, S, & Fine, M, 'Bereavement Following the Death of a Child', *Contemporary Family Therapy*, 1987, Vol. 9, No. 3.

Vanstone, W, *Love's Endeavour, Love's Expense*, Darton, Longman & Todd, London.

Videka-Sherman, L, 'Coping with the Death of a Child', *American Journal of Orthopsychiatry*, 1982, Vol. 52.

Walter, T, *Funerals*, Hodder & Stoughton, London, 1990.

Wiesbe, W, *Why us?*, IVP, Leicester, 1984.

Wilson, A, et al, 'The Death of the Newborn Twin: An Analysis of Parental Bereavement', *Pediatrics*, 1982, Vol. 70.

Wolterstorff, N, *Lament for a Son*, Eerdmans, Grand Rapids, 1987.

Worden, J, *Grief Counselling and Grief Therapy*, Tavistock, London, 1983.

Index

PRIORITY ORDER FORM

Please send me _____ copies of Suffering Love at £7.50 per copy.
P&P is £1.50 for the first copy and 50p per copy thereafter.

Total cost of books: £ _____
Total P&P charge: £ _____
TOTAL COST: £ _____

Please tick *one* method of payment:

☐ I enclose a cheque/PO payable to Advantage for £ _____
☐ Please debit my Visa/Mastercard/Delta number:

Expiry date: _____ Signature _____

Name: _____

Address: _____

_____ Post Code: _____ Daytime Phone: _____

▲DVANTAGE

Advantage, The Town House, 46 Radford Road, Leamington Spa CV31 1LZ
Phone/Fax: 01926 451521   E.Mail 100657.307@CompuServe.COM